Best

TABLETOP Quilts

FONS & PORTER STAFF
Editors-in-Chief Marianne Fons and Liz Porter

Editor Jean Nolte
Assistant Editor Diane Tomlinson
Managing Editor Debra Finan
Technical Writer Kristine Peterson

Art Director Tony Jacobson

Editorial Assistant Cinde Alexander
Sewing Specialist Cindy Hathaway

Contributing Photographers Craig Anderson, Dean Tanner, Katie Downey
Contributing Photo Assistant DeElda Wittmack

Publisher Kristi Loeffelholz
Advertising Manager Cristy Adamski
Retail Manager Sharon Hart
Web Site Manager Phillip Zacharias
Customer Service Manager Tiffiny Bond
Staff Peggy Garner, Shelle Goodwin, Kimberly Romero, Laura Saner, Karol Skeffington, Yvonne Smith, Natalie Wakeman, Anne Welker, Karla Wesselmann

New Track Media LLC
President and CEO Stephen J. Kent
Chief Financial Officer Mark F. Arnett
President, Book Publishing W. Budge Wallis
Vice President/Publishing Director Joel P. Toner
Vice President Consumer Marketing Dennis O'Brien
Vice President, Production & Technology Derek W. Corson
Circulation Susan Sidler
IT Manager Denise Donnarumma
Group Marketing Manager Nicole McGuire
New Business Manager Lance Covert

Our Mission Statement
Our goal is for you to enjoy making quilts as much as we do.

LEISURE ARTS STAFF
Editor-in-Chief Susan White Sullivan
Quilt and Craft Publications Director Cheryl Johnson
Special Projects Director Susan Frantz Wiles
Senior Prepress Director Mark Hawkins
Imaging Technician Stephanie Johnson
Publishing Systems Administrator Becky Riddle
Mac Information Technology Specialist Robert Young

President and Chief Executive Officer Rick Barton
Vice President and Chief Operations Officer Tom Siebenmorgen
Vice President of Sales Mike Behar
Director of Finance and Administration Laticia Mull Dittrich
National Sales Director Martha Adams
Creative Services Chaska Lucas
Information Technology Director Hermine Linz
Controller Francis Caple
Vice President, Operations Jim Dittrich
Retail Customer Service Manager Stan Raynor
Print Production Manager Fred F. Pruss

Library of Congress Control Number: 2010939696
ISBN-13/EAN: 978-1-60900-109-4

Table toppers are the perfect quilted treasures for your home. This special collection of projects we've hand picked for you includes a variety of styles and sizes—some of our best-ever tabletop quilts—for every season of the year. Enjoy the beautiful photography as you browse through the pages to find the one that's just right for you. We've included patterns for all skill levels, and some include *Sew Easy* lessons that will guide you via step-by-step photography through any project-specific special techniques. Choose your favorite pattern and fabrics, and stitch a tabletop quilt to enhance your home décor.

Happy Quilting,

Marianne & Liz

Spring

Summer

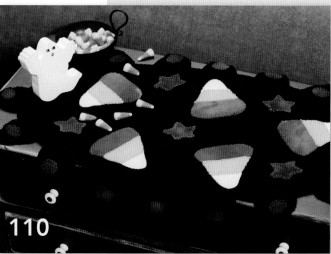

Fall

Winter

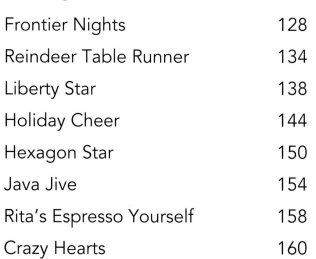

Spring

Chicken Dance

This clever table topper is perfect for spring with its cute dancing chicks. See *Sew Easy: Cutting Large Circles* on page 13 for instructions to cut the background and center pieces.

PROJECT RATING: INTERMEDIATE

Size: 41½" Diameter

MATERIALS

⅜ yard each of 2 red prints and 2 yellow prints

¾ yard red chick print

1¾ yards yellow check

⅜ yard red-and-white stripe

½" Bias Tape Maker (optional)

Paper-backed fusible web

1¼ yards backing fabric

42" square batting

Cutting

Measurements include ¼" seam allowances. Patterns for Wedge and appliqué are on page 12. Follow manufacturer's instructions for using fusible web. See *Sew Easy: Cutting Large Circles* on page 13 for instructions for cutting A and B circles.

From assorted red and yellow prints, cut a total of:

• 20 Wedges.

• 7 Chicks.

• 6 Chicks reversed.

• 18 Wings.

From red-and-white stripe, cut:

• 120" of (1"-wide) bias strips. Join to make continuous bias. Press both long edges to center, wrong sides facing, or use Bias Tape Maker to prepare bias strip.

From red chick print, cut:

• 1 (11") square. From square, cut 10"-diameter A Circle.

• 2 (2½"-wide) strips. From strips, cut 32 (2½") C squares.

• 6 Wedges.

• 3 Chicks.

• 2 Chicks reversed.

From yellow check, cut:

• 1 (42") square. From square, cut 41"-diameter B Circle.

• 2 (2½"-wide) strips. From strips, cut 32 (2½") C squares.

• 6 Wedges.

From backing, cut:

• 1 (42") square.

Quilt Assembly

1. Lay out 32 assorted red and yellow print Wedges as shown in *Quilt Top Assembly Diagram*. Join to make pieced ring.

2. Center pieced ring on yellow check B circle. Pin in place. Pin red A circle in center, overlapping pieced ring.

3. Center red-and-white stripe bias strip over edge of A circle; pin in place. Appliqué or topstitch edges of bias strip.

4. Center red-and-white stripe bias strip over outer edge of pieced circle; pin in place. Appliqué or topstitch edges of bias strip.

> ## Sew **Smart**™
> Baste outer edge of pieced circle to yellow check circle and add bias strips after spokes are quilted. —Marianne

5. Referring to photo on page 11, arrange Chicks and Wings atop quilt top; fuse in place.

6. Machine appliqué Chicks and Wings using yellow thread and blanket stitch as shown in *Embroidery Diagram*. Stitch feet using short, narrow zigzag stitch and orange thread. Stitch eyes using Satin Stitch and black thread (*Satin Stitch Diagram*).

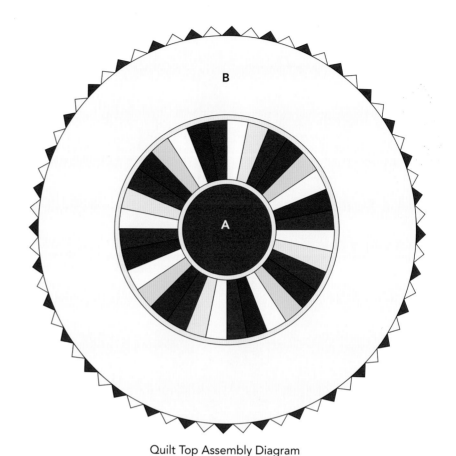

Quilt Top Assembly Diagram

Satin Stitch

Prairie Point Placement Diagram

7. Fold 1 yellow check C square in half; fold in half again to make 1 Prairie Point (*Prairie Point Diagrams*). Press. Make 32 yellow check and 32 red chick print Prairie Points.

Prairie Point Diagrams

8. Evenly space Prairie Points around perimeter of quilt top, aligning raw edges as shown in *Prairie Point Placement Diagram*. Pin; baste in place.

> ## Sew **Smart**™
> Fold quilt top in quarters and crease folds for spacing Prairie Points. Place 16 points in each quarter. —Marianne

Finishing

1. Place backing, right side up, atop batting. Layer quilt top atop backing, right sides facing. Stitch around edge, leaving a 10" opening for turning. Trim backing and batting even with edge of quilt top.

2. Turn right side out through opening. Press. Whipstitch opening closed.

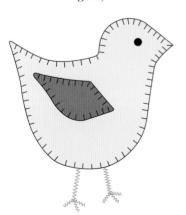

Embroidery Diagram

3. Topstitch ¼" inside edge of outer ring.

4. Quilt as desired. Quilt shown was quilted with meandering in the center, in the ditch of the wedges, and with "spokes" in the outer ring *(Quilting Diagram).*

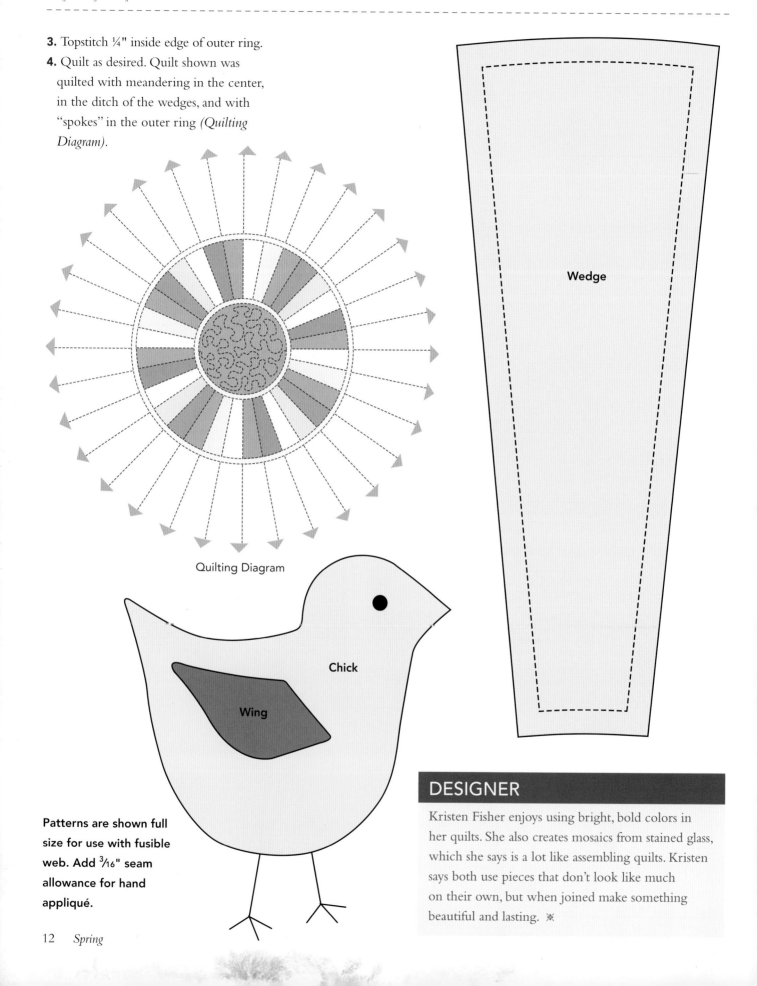

Quilting Diagram

Wedge

Chick

Wing

Patterns are shown full size for use with fusible web. Add ³⁄₁₆" seam allowance for hand appliqué.

DESIGNER

Kristen Fisher enjoys using bright, bold colors in her quilts. She also creates mosaics from stained glass, which she says is a lot like assembling quilts. Kristen says both use pieces that don't look like much on their own, but when joined make something beautiful and lasting. ✳

Cutting Large Circles

Make perfect circles of any size using these easy-to-follow instructions.

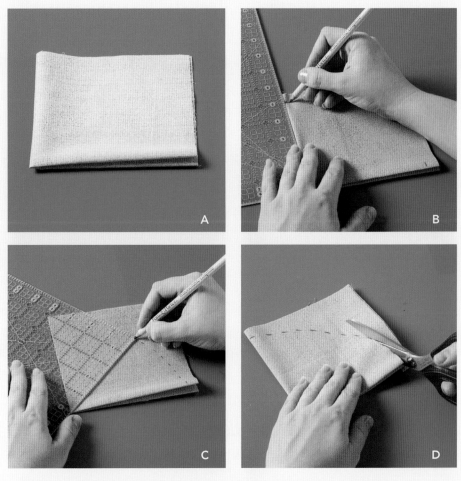

1. Determine diameter of desired circle and cut a square slightly larger than that measurement.
2. Fold square into quarters (*Photo A*).
3. Divide circle diameter measurement in half to determine radius of circle. Measure from inner point of square and make mark on both edges (*Photo B*).
4. Rotate ruler and make additional marks (*Photo C*).
5. Cut folded square along marks (*Photo D*).

Tea Time

This adorable table topper or wallhanging was designed by Rachel Shelburne, and was made by her mother, Darlene Zimmerman. Enjoy a cup of tea while you make this fun quilt.

PROJECT RATING: EASY

Size: 30" × 34½"

Blocks: 3 (7½" × 10½") Teapot blocks
3 (4½" × 6") Cup blocks

MATERIALS

7 fat quarters★ assorted red, yellow, and blue prints

⅝ yard blue solid for borders and binding

½ yard white print for background

Paper-backed fusible web

3 (¾"-diameter) buttons

Black embroidery floss

1 yard backing fabric

Crib-size quilt batting

★fat quarter = 18" × 20"

Cutting

Measurements include ¼" seam allowances. Border strips are exact length needed. You may want to make them longer to allow for piecing variations. Patterns for appliqué are on page 17. Follow manufacturer's instructions for using fusible web.

From each fat quarter, cut:

• 3 (2"-wide) strips. From strips, cut 30 (2") A squares. (You will have a few extra.)

• 1 (3½"-wide) strip. From strip, cut 2 (3½") B squares.

From remainder of each of 3 fat quarters, cut:

• 3 Cups.

• 3 Cup Handles.

• 3 Cup Bases.

From remainder of each of 3 fat quarters, cut:

• 3 Teapots.

• 3 Teapot Handles.

• 3 Teapot Bases.

• 3 Lids.

From blue solid, cut:

• 4 (2¼"-wide) strips for binding.

• 4 (2"-wide) strips. From strips, cut 2 (2" × 27½") top and bottom inner borders and 2 (2" × 29") side inner borders.

From white print, cut:

• 1 (8"-wide) strip. From strip, cut 3 (8" × 11") rectangles.

• 1 (5"-wide) strip. From strip, cut 3 (5" × 6½") rectangles.

Block Assembly

1. Referring to *Teapot Block Diagram*, position 1 Teapot, 1 Teapot Base, 1 Lid, and 1 Teapot Handle atop 1 (8" × 11") white print background rectangle. Fuse pieces in place.

Teapot Block Diagram

2. Using 3 strands of black embroidery floss, blanket stitch around each appliqué piece to complete block *(Blanket Stitch Diagram)*. Make 3 Teapot blocks.

Blanket Stitch Diagram

3. Referring to *Cup Block Diagram*, position 1 Cup, 1 Cup Base, and 1 Cup Handle atop 1 (5" × 6½") white print background rectangle. Fuse in place.

Cup Block Diagram

4. Using black thread, blanket stitch around each appliqué to complete block. Make 3 Cup blocks.

Quilt Assembly

1. Referring to *Quilt Top Assembly Diagram*, lay out appliqué blocks, A squares, and B squares. Join into segments as shown. Join blocks and segments into rows; join rows to complete quilt center.

2. Add side inner borders to quilt center. Add top and bottom inner borders to quilt.

3. Join 21 (2") squares to make 1 side outer border. Make 2 side outer borders. Add borders to quilt.

4. Join 20 (2") squares to make 1 top border. Repeat to make bottom border. Add borders to quilt.

Finishing

1. Layer backing, batting, and quilt top; baste. Quilt as desired. Quilt shown was outline quilted around teapots and cups, and is stitched in the ditch around each A square. The blue border has a small wave pattern.

2. Join 2¼"-wide blue strips into 1 continuous piece for straight-grain French-fold binding. Add binding to quilt.

3. Sew 1 button to each teapot lid.

Quilt Top Assembly Diagram

TRIED & TRUE

Try Asian inspired fabrics such as these for a rich, more formal look.

DESIGNER

Darlene Zimmerman's grandmother was a quilter, and her mother sewed garments for her six daughters and taught them all to sew their own clothing. When Darlene had children of her own, she took up quilting as a hobby, and it quickly turned into a business. She lectures and teaches nationwide, has designed quilting tools and fabric lines, and published many quilting books.

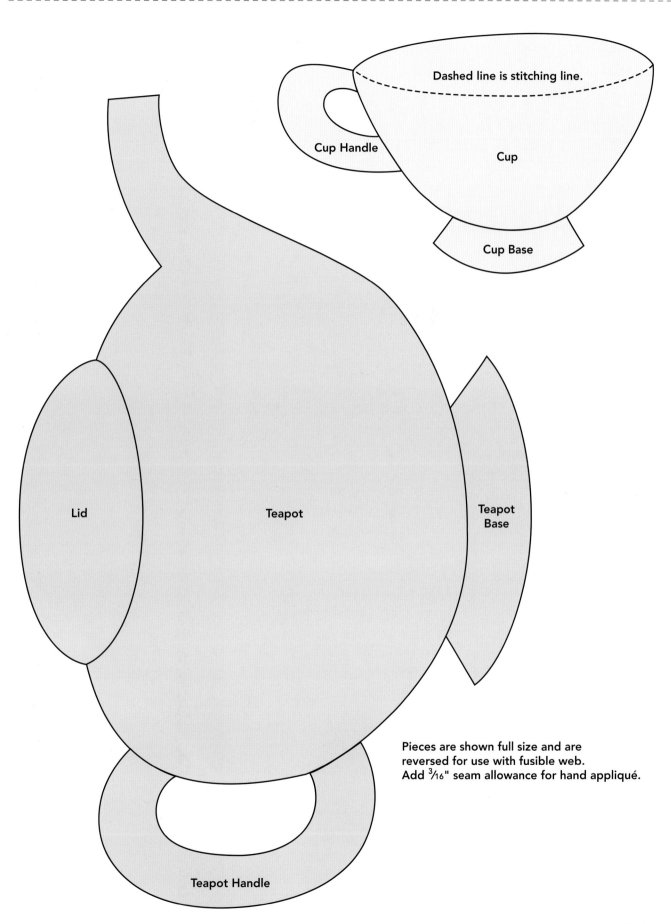

Dashed line is stitching line.

Cup Handle

Cup

Cup Base

Lid

Teapot

Teapot Base

Pieces are shown full size and are reversed for use with fusible web. Add ³⁄₁₆" seam allowance for hand appliqué.

Teapot Handle

PROJECT DESIGNED BY **Marianne Fons and Liz Porter**.
MADE BY **Cindy Hathaway**.

Spring Fling

This table runner in fresh new prints is a lovely accent for your home.
Easy diagonal seam piecing makes this project simple and quick.

Size: 18" × 45"
Blocks: 8 (4½" × 9") Leaf blocks
8 (4½") Flower blocks

MATERIALS

½ yard pink stripe
½ yard cream floral
¼ yard green print
½ yard pink print
1 fat eighth★ yellow print
1⅜ yards backing fabric
Crib size quilt batting
★fat eighth = 9" × 20"

Cutting

Measurements include ¼" seam allowances. Border strips are exact length needed. You may want to make them longer to allow for piecing variations.

From pink stripe, cut:
- 4 (2¼"-wide) strips for binding.
- 3 (1½"-wide) strips. From strips, cut 2 (1½" × 34½") top and bottom inner borders and 2 (1½" × 9½") side inner borders.

From cream floral, cut:
- 3 (2½"-wide) strips. From strips, cut 32 (2½") B squares and 16 (2½" × 1½") C rectangles.
- 2 (2"-wide) strips. From strips, cut 32 (2") E squares.
- 3 (1½"-wide) strips. From strips, cut 64 (1½") A squares.

From green print, cut:
- 2 (2½"-wide) strips. From strips, cut 32 (2½") B squares.
- 2 (1"-wide) strips. From strips, cut 8 (1" × 9½") D rectangles.

From pink print, cut:
- 1 (7½"-wide) strip. From strip, cut 1 (7½" × 34½") rectangle for center.
- 3 (2"-wide) strips. From strips, cut 16 (2" × 5") F rectangles and 16 (2") E squares.

From yellow print, cut:
- 1 (2"-wide) strip. From strip, cut 8 (2") E squares.

Block Assembly

1. Referring to *Diagonal Seams Diagrams,* place 1 cream floral A square atop 1 green print B square, right sides facing. Stitch diagonally from corner to corner as shown. Trim ¼" beyond stitching. Press open to reveal triangle. Repeat for opposite corner to complete 1 Leaf Unit. Make 32 Leaf Units.

Diagonal Seams Diagrams

2. Referring to *Leaf Block Assembly Diagrams,* lay out 4 Leaf Units, 4 cream floral B squares, 2 cream floral C rectangles, and 1 green print D rectangle. Join into rows; join rows to complete 1 Leaf block. Make 8 Leaf blocks.

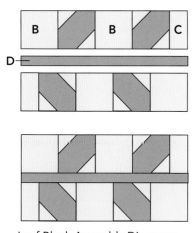

Leaf Block Assembly Diagrams

3. Using diagonal seams method, add 1 cream floral E square to each end of 1 pink print F rectangle to make 1 Flower Unit *(Flower Unit Diagrams).* Make 16 Flower Units.

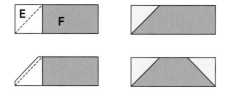

Flower Unit Diagrams

4. Referring to *Flower Block Assembly Diagram,* lay out 2 Flower Units, 2 pink print E squares, and 1 yellow print E square. Join squares to make center row; join flower units and center row to complete 1 Flower block *(Flower Block Diagram).* Make 8 Flower blocks.

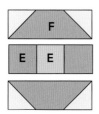

Flower Block Assembly Diagram

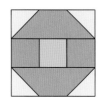

Flower Block Diagram

Quilt Assembly

1. Referring to *Quilt Top Assembly Diagram,* add pink stripe top and bottom inner borders to pink print center rectangle. Add pink stripe side inner borders to center.

2. Join 2 Flower blocks and 3 Leaf blocks to make top outer border. Repeat for bottom outer border. Add borders to quilt.

3. Join 2 Flower blocks and 1 Leaf block to make side outer border. Make 2 side outer borders. Add borders to quilt.

Finishing

1. Layer backing, batting, and quilt top; baste. Quilt as desired. Quilt shown was quilted in the ditch.

2. Join 2¼"-wide pink stripe strips into 1 continuous piece for straight-grain French-fold binding. Add binding to quilt.

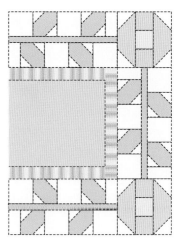

Quilting Diagram

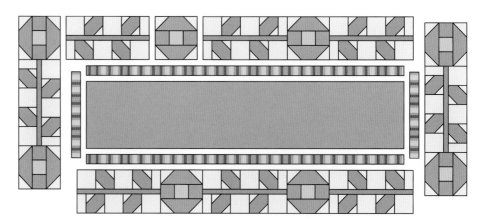

Quilt Top Assembly Diagram

TRIED & TRUE

For a country look, we
used prints from the Killean
collection by RJR Fabrics. ✳

PROJECTS BY **Rhoda Nelson**.
MACHINE QUILTED BY **Vicki Stratton**.

Granny's Kitchen

Your kitchen or dining room will look charming with this matching set.
Try our easy technique for making Dresden Plate wedges, and
you'll have your projects done in no time!

Wallhanging/Table Topper

PROJECT RATING: CHALLENGING

Size: 41⅜" × 41⅜"

Blocks: 1 (16¾") Dresden Plate block and 4 (4¾") Fan blocks

MATERIALS

1¼ yards white solid for background

1 fat eighth★ pink print #1 for quilt center

6 fat quarters★★ assorted prints in pink, blue, green, purple, yellow, and white
for wedges and pieced borders

1 yard pink print for outer border and binding

¼ yard blue print for border and Corner blocks

¼ yard green print for border

¼ yard yellow print for border

2¾ yards backing fabric

Crib-size quilt batting

★fat eighth = 9" × 20"

★★fat quarter = 18" × 20"

Cutting

Measurements include ¼" seam allowances. Border strips are exact length needed. You may want to make them longer to allow for piecing variations. Patterns for Wedges, Circle, and Quarter Circle are on page 29.

From white solid, cut:
- 1 (17¼"-wide) strip. From strip, cut 1 (17¼") background square.
- 1 (5¼"-wide) strip. From strip, cut 4 (5¼") F squares and 2 (4") squares. Cut (4") squares in half diagonally to make 4 half-square E triangles.
- 1 (4⅜"-wide) strip. From strip, cut 5 (4⅜") squares. Cut squares in half diagonally in both directions to make 20 quarter-square A triangles.
- 2 (4¼"-wide) strips. From strips, cut 16 (4¼") squares. Cut squares in half diagonally in both directions to make 64 quarter-square C triangles.
- 1 (2⅜"-wide) strip. From strip, cut 8 (2⅜") squares. Cut squares in half diagonally to make 16 half-square D triangles.

From pink print fat eighth, cut:
- 1 Circle.

From each fat quarter, cut:
- 1 (2⅝"-wide) strip. From strip, cut 6 (2⅝") B squares.
- 1 (4⅜") square. Cut square in half diagonally in both directions to make 4 quarter-square A triangles.
- 4 Large Wedges.
- 4 Small Wedges.

From pink print, cut:
- 4 (5¼"-wide) strips. From strips, cut 4 (5¼" × 32⅜") border #6.
- 5 (2¼"-wide) strips for binding.

From blue print, cut:

- 4 (1½"-wide) strips. From strips, cut 2 (1½" × 17¼") side border #1 and 2 (1½" × 19¼") top and bottom border #1.
- 4 Quarter Circles.

From green print, cut:

- 4 (1½"-wide) strips. From strips, cut 2 (1½" × 30⅜") side border #5 and 2 (1½" × 32⅜") top and bottom border #5.

From yellow print, cut:

- 4 (1½"-wide) strips. From strips, cut 2 (1½" × 24½") top and bottom border #3 and 2 (1½" × 22½") side border #3.

Quilt Center Assembly

1. Fold 1 Large Wedge in half lengthwise, right sides facing. Stitch across top as shown in *Stitching Diagram*. Trim corner.

Stitching Diagram

2. Open seam and turn point right side out. Press, centering seam as shown in *Wedge Diagram*. Make 24 Large Wedges.

Wedge Diagram

3. Join 6 Wedges to make a Wedge Unit as shown in *Plate Assembly Diagrams*. Make 4 Wedge Units.

4. Join Wedge Units to complete 1 Dresden Plate. Turn Dresden Plate wrong side up and press seams open, being careful not to stretch fabric.

Wedge Unit

Plate Assembly Diagrams

Border #2 Diagrams

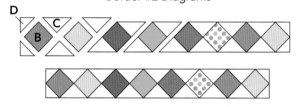

Side Border #4 Diagrams

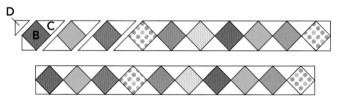

Bottom Border #4 Diagrams

5. Referring to *Quilt Top Assembly Diagram*, center Dresden Plate and pink print circle on white background square; pin in place. Appliqué points of plate. Turn under seam allowance as you appliqué circle in place to complete quilt center.

Pieced Border Assembly

1. Lay out 6 print A triangles and 5 white solid A triangles as shown in *Border #2 Diagrams*. Join to complete 1 border #2. Make 4 border #2.

2. Lay out 8 print B squares, 14 white solid C triangles, and 4 white solid D triangles as shown in *Side Border #4 Diagrams*. Join into diagonal rows; join rows to complete 1 side border #4. Make 2 side border #4.

3. Lay out 10 print B squares, 18 white solid C triangles, and 4 white solid D triangles as shown in *Bottom Border #4 Diagrams*. Join into diagonal rows; join rows to complete bottom border #4. Repeat for top border #4.

Corner Block Assembly

1. Make 20 Small Wedges as before.

2. Join 5 Small Wedges as shown in *Fan Diagram*. Make 4 Fans.

Fan Diagram

3. Pin 1 Fan atop 1 white solid F square, aligning raw edges of Fan with sides of square as shown in *Corner Block Assembly Diagram*. Appliqué Fan points on square.

Corner Block
Assembly Diagram

Corner Block
Diagram

4. Turn under curved edge of Quarter Circle and appliqué on fan to complete 1 Corner block *(Corner Block Diagram)*. Make 4 Corner blocks.

Quilt Assembly

1. Add 1 side border #1 to each side of quilt center. Add top and bottom border #1 to quilt center.

2. Add 1 border #2 to each side of quilt. Add 1 white solid E triangle to each corner.

3. Add 1 side border #3 to each side of quilt. Add top and bottom border #3 to quilt. Repeat for borders #4 and #5.

4. Add 1 border #6 to each side of quilt. Add 1 Corner block to each end of remaining borders. Add borders to top and bottom of quilt.

Finishing

1. Divide backing into 2 (1⅜-yard) lengths. Cut 1 piece in half lengthwise to make 2 narrow panels. Join 1 narrow panel to wider panel. Remaining panel is extra and can be used to make a hanging sleeve.

2. Layer backing, batting, and quilt top; baste. Quilt as desired. Quilt shown was quilted with an allover loopy design in quilt center and with meandering flowers in outer border *(Quilting Diagram)*.

Quilt Top Assembly Diagram

3. Join 2¼"-wide pink print strips into 1 continuous piece for straight-grain French-fold binding. Add binding to quilt.

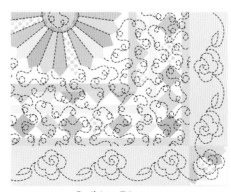

Quilting Diagram

TRIED & TRUE

We used Vine Creek prints by Kansas Troubles for Moda to give our version a rustic, country look.

Table Runner

PROJECT RATING: INTERMEDIATE

Size: 12" × 38½"

MATERIALS

½ yard white solid for background

5 fat eighths★ assorted prints in pink, blue, green, purple, and yellow for wedges and pieced borders

1 fat quarter★★ pink print for triangles

1 fat eighth★ green print for borders

¼ yard blue print for binding

½ yard backing fabric

Craft-size quilt batting

★fat eighth = 9" × 20"

★★fat quarter = 18" × 20"

Cutting

Measurements include ¼" seam allowances. Pattern for Large Wedge is on page 29.

From white solid, cut:

• 1 (12½"-wide) strip. From strip, cut 1 (12½" × 18½") background A rectangle.

• 1 (4¼"-wide) strip. From strip, cut 3 (4¼") squares and 4 (2⅜") squares. Cut 4¼" squares in half diagonally in both directions to make 12 quarter-square C triangles. Cut 2⅜" squares in half diagonally to make 8 half-square D triangles.

From fat eighths, cut a total of:

• 10 Wedges.

• 8 (2⅜") B squares.

From pink print fat quarter, cut:

• 1 (9⅜"-wide) strip. From strip, cut 1 (9⅜") square. Cut square in half diagonally to make 2 half-square E triangles.

From green print fat eighth, cut:

• 4 (1⅛"-wide) strips. From strips, cut 4 (1⅛" × 12½") rectangles.

From blue print, cut:

• 3 (2¼"-wide) strips for binding.

Table Runner Center Assembly

1. Fold 1 Wedge in half lengthwise, right sides facing. Stitch across top as shown in *Stitching Diagram*. Trim corner.

Stitching Diagram

2. Open seam and turn point right side out. Press, centering seam as shown in *Wedge Diagram*. Make 10 Wedges.

Wedge Diagram

3. Join 5 Wedges as shown in *Fan Diagram*. Make 2 Fans.

Fan Diagram

4. Place Fans wrong side up and press seams open, being careful not to stretch fabric.

5. Referring to *Table Runner Assembly Diagram*, center Fans on white background rectangle, pin in place. Appliqué Fans on rectangle, turning under curved edge and sides, to complete table runner center.

Pieced Border Assembly

1. Lay out 4 print B squares, 6 white solid C triangles, and 4 white solid D triangles as shown in *Border Digrams*.

2. Join into diagonal rows; join rows to complete 1 pieced border. Make 2 pieced borders.

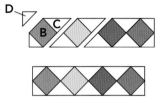

Border Diagrams

Quilt Assembly

1. Lay out table runner center, green print rectangles, pieced borders, and pink print E triangles as shown in *Table Runner Assembly Diagram*.

2. Join to complete table runner.

Finishing

1. Layer backing, batting, and table runner top; baste. Quilt as desired. Quilt shown was quilted with allover swirls and loops *(Quilting Diagram)*.

2. Join 2¼"-wide blue print strips into 1 continuous piece for straight-grain French-fold binding. Add binding to quilt.

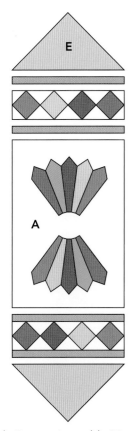

Table Runner Assembly Diagram

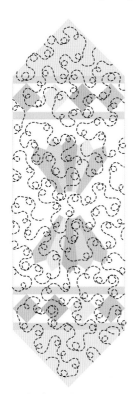

Quilting Diagram

Apron

PROJECT RATING: EASY

MATERIALS

1⅛ yards pink print for skirt

⅜ yard cream solid for bib

5 (3" × 6") rectangles assorted
prints for fan

1 (6" × 6¾") rectangle green print
for pocket

Cutting

Measurements include ¼" seam allowances. Pattern for Large Wedge is on page 29.

From pink print, cut:

• 1 (25"-wide) strip. From strip, cut
1 (25") square and 2 (25" × 3") strips.

• 3 (4½"-wide) strips. From strips, cut
2 (4½" × 34") strips.

• 1 (2½"-wide) strip. From strip, cut
2 (2½" × 18½") strips.

From cream solid, cut:

• 1 (11¾"-wide) strip. From strip, cut
2 (11¾") squares.

From each print rectangle, cut:

• 1 Large Wedge.

Strap Assembly

1. Fold 1 (4½"-wide) pink print strip in half lengthwise. Stitch down one side and across end. Repeat for remaining 4½"-wide strip (waist ties) and 3"-wide strips (neck ties). Turn strips right side out; press.

Bib Assembly

1. Fold 1 Wedge in half lengthwise, right sides facing. Stitch across top as shown in *Stitching Diagram*. Trim corner.

Stitching Diagram

2. Open seam and turn point right side out. Press, centering seam as shown in *Wedge Diagram*. Make 5 Wedges.

Wedge Diagram

3. Join 5 Wedges as shown in *Fan Diagram*.

Fan Diagram

4. Press seam allowances of fan toward wrong side. Center fan on 1 cream square; appliqué in place.

5. Pin neck ties to top of bib front, 1½" from side edges as shown in *Bib Assembly Diagrams* on page 28. Place remaining cream square atop bib front, right sides facing. Stitch sides and top, rounding top corners. Trim corners, turn right side out; press.

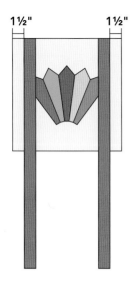

1½"　　1½"

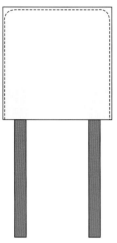

Bib Assembly Diagrams

Skirt Assembly

1. Press ⅜" side seam allowances toward wrong side of pink square. Press ⅜" toward wrong side again. Topstitch side hems along folded edge.

2. Press bottom edge of square ¼" toward wrong side. Press 3" hem toward wrong side. Topstitch hem along folded edge.

3. Press top edge of green print rectangle ¼" toward wrong side. Press 1" hem toward wrong side. Topstitch hem along folded edge. Press sides and bottom ½" toward wrong side.

4. Position pocket on skirt 4½" away from side edge and 9½" from bottom edge. Top stitch sides and bottom of pocket.

5. Stitch 2 gathering lines of machine basting along top of apron skirt, placing them ⅛" and ⅜" from top edge.

Apron Assembly

1. Pin bib to 1 (2½" × 18½") pink print waistband strip, right sides facing. Center waist ties on ends of strip, aligning raw edges.

2. Place remaining 2½" × 18½" pink print strip atop first strip. Stitch ends and top, enclosing bib and ties in seam. Turn right side out; press.

3. Pin skirt to waistband front, right sides facing and keeping waistband lining free. Adjust gathers to fit waistband. Stitch skirt to waistband. Press seam allowance toward waistband.

Sew Smart™

You can tell which side is the waistband front by looking for right side of bib. —Liz

4. Fold seam allowance of waistband lining to wrong side and slipstitch folded edge to apron, covering stitching.

DESIGNER

Rhoda Nelson is a professional quiltmaker and designer who works with RJR Fabrics to create original quilts and projects showcasing new fabrics. ✳

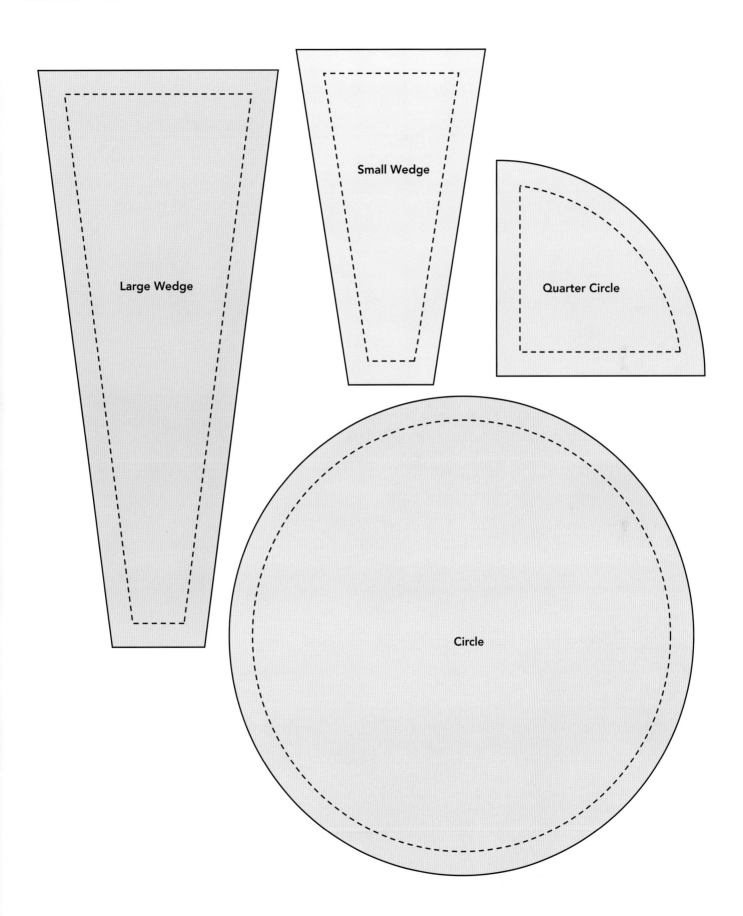

Large Wedge

Small Wedge

Quarter Circle

Circle

May Baskets

Designer Glenna Hailey created her *May Baskets* wallhanging using the Fun with Feedsacks fabric collection she designed for P&B Textiles. Embellished with rickrack, this project is a quick fix for a drab wall or table.

PROJECT RATING: INTERMEDIATE
Size: 36" × 36"
Blocks: 4 (12") Basket blocks

MATERIALS

⅞ yard yellow check for border
⅜ yard light yellow solid for basket background
20 (9") squares assorted red, purple, blue, and pink prints
  for blocks
1 fat eighth★ each red, purple, blue, and pink solid for
  block frames and baskets
1 fat eighth★ yellow solid for flower centers
1 fat eighth★ green solid for leaves
1¼ yards each red, purple, blue, and pink rickrack
Paper-backed fusible web
Template material
Optional—Pinking shears or rotary cutter with pinking
  blade
⅜ yard bright print for binding
1¼ yards backing fabric
Crib-size quilt batting
★fat eighth = 9" × 20"

Cutting

Measurements include ¼" seam allowances. Patterns for appliqué pieces are on page 35. Follow manufacturer's instructions for using fusible web. Border strips are exact length needed. You may want to make them longer to allow for piecing variations.

From yellow check, cut:

- 4 (6½"-wide) strips. From strips, cut 2 (6½" x 36½") top and bottom borders and 2 (6½" x 24½") side borders.

From light yellow solid, cut:

- 1 (6⅛"-wide) strip. From strip, cut 2 (6⅛") squares. Cut squares in half diagonally to make 4 half-square A triangles.
- 1 (3⅜"-wide) strip. From strip, cut 2 (3⅜") squares. Cut squares in half diagonally to make 4 half-square D triangles.
- 1 (1¾"-wide) strip. From strip, cut 8 (1¾" × 4½") C rectangles.

From each of 4 (9") print squares, cut:

- 1 (6⅛") square. Cut square in half diagonally to make 2 half-square A triangles. (One triangle of each fabric is extra and can be used for flower.)

From each of 16 (9") print squares, cut:

- 1 (6⅞") square. Cut square in half diagonally to make 2 half-square G triangles. (One triangle of each fabric is extra and can be used for flower.)
- 1 Flower.

From each red, purple, blue, and pink solid fat eighth, cut:

- 2 (1½"-wide) strips. From strips, cut 2 (1½" × 9") F rectangles and 2 (1½" × 7") E rectangles.
- 1 (2⅛") square. Cut square in half diagonally to make 2 half-square B triangles.

From yellow solid, cut:

- 16 Stars.

From green solid, cut:

- 32 Leaves. If desired, cut one edge with pinking shears or rotary cutter with pinking blade.

From each color of rickrack, cut:

- 1 (34"-long) piece for border.
- 1 (8"-long) piece for handle.

From bright print, cut:

- 4 (2¼"-wide) strips for binding.

Basket Assembly

1. Make template from Handle Placement Guide on page 35. Center and mark handle placement line on 1 light yellow A triangle. Attach 8" length of rickrack to marked line. Stitch through the center of rickrack or appliqué the edges using matching thread.

2. Lay out 1 print A triangle, 2 matching B triangles, 1 light yellow A triangle with rickrack handle attached, 2 light yellow C rectangles, and 1 light yellow D triangle as shown in *Basket Assembly Diagrams.* Join to make basket.

3. Choose a matching set of 2 E rectangles and 2 F rectangles. Referring to *Block Assembly Diagram,* add E rectangles to 2 opposite sides of basket; add F rectangles to remaining 2 sides.

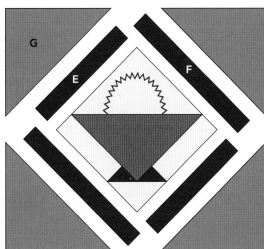

Block Assembly Diagram

4. Choose 4 G triangles to coordinate with basket. Add 1 triangle to each side of basket to complete Basket block *(Block Diagram).* Make 4 Basket blocks.

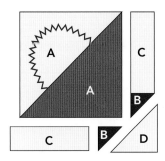

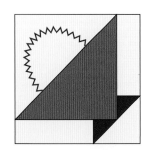

Basket Assembly Diagrams

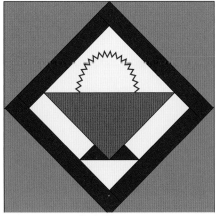

Block Diagram

Quilt Top Assembly

1. Lay out Basket Blocks as shown in *Quilt Top Assembly Diagram.*

2. Join into horizontal rows; join rows to complete quilt center.

Quilt Top Assembly Diagram

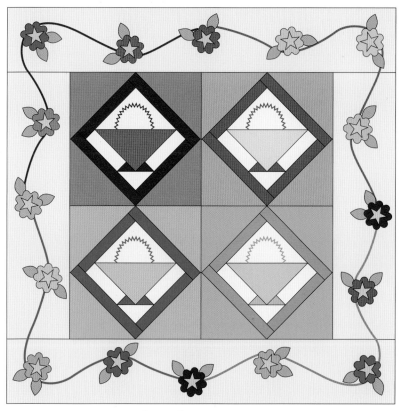

Appliqué Placement Diagram

3. Add side borders to quilt center. Add top and bottom borders to quilt.

4. Referring to photo on page 34 and Appliqué Placement Diagram arrange rickrack, leaves, and flowers on border. Appliqué pieces in place.

Finishing

1. Layer backing, batting, and quilt top; baste. Quilt as desired. Quilt shown was quilted with an overall freehand design.

2. Join 2¼"-wide bright print strips into 1 continuous piece for straight-grain French-fold binding. Add binding to quilt.

TRIED & TRUE

Use bright, fun prints like these from the Summer Fun collection by Carol Eldridge for P&B Textiles. Create the handle from a bias strip instead of rickrack for a different look.

DESIGNER

A quilter for over 20 years, Glenna Hailey worked and taught in quilt shops prior to developing her line of feedsack-inspired patterns. A collector of antiques, vintage fabrics, and original feedsacks, Glenna built a collection of over 2000 feedsacks before she decided it was time to combine her quilting experience and her vast collection, and Hollyhock Quilts was born.

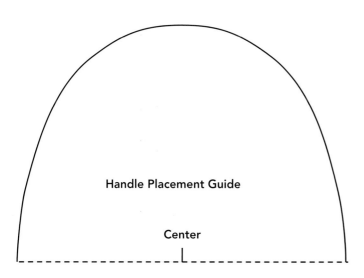

Handle Placement Guide

Center

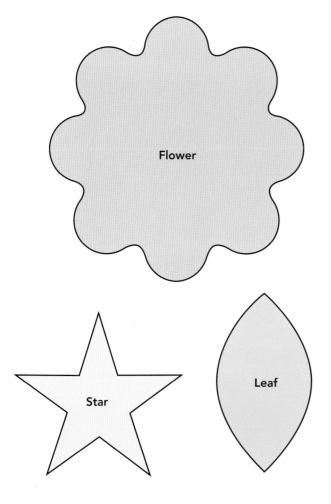

Flower

Star

Leaf

Patterns are shown full size for use with fusible
web. Add $^3/_{16}$" seam allowance for hand appliqué.

PROJECT BY **Judy Flanagan**.

Pineapple Picnic

Designer Judy Flanagan combined paper foundation piecing and
fusible appliqué to make this sunshiny table topper.

PROJECT RATING: CHALLENGING

Size: 30" × 30"

Blocks: 25 (4") Pineapple blocks

MATERIALS

⅜ yard yellow solid for block centers and inner border

1⅛ yards cream solid for blocks and outer border

⅜ yard yellow print for binding and pineapples

⅜ yard green solid for vines and leaves

16 fat eighths★ assorted 1930s reproduction prints in red, yellow, green, blue, lavender, and pink for blocks and border appliqué

1 yard backing fabric

Crib-size quilt batting

Tracing paper

Paper-backed fusible web

★fat eighth = 9" × 20"

Cutting

Pattern for paper foundation piecing is on page 38. Measurements include ¼" seam allowances. Border strips are exact length needed. You may want to make them longer to allow for piecing variations. Follow manufacturer's instructions for using fusible web. Refer to *Sew Easy: Paper Foundation Piecing* on page 39 for instructions on making blocks.

From yellow solid, cut:

- 2 (1¾"-wide) strips. From strips, cut 25 (1¾") C squares for block centers.
- 4 (1½"-wide) strips. From strips, cut 2 (1½" × 22½") top and bottom inner borders and 2 (1½" × 20½") side inner borders.

Quilt Top Assembly Diagram

From cream solid, cut:

- 4 (4½"-wide) strips. From strips, cut 2 (4½" × 30½") top and bottom outer borders and 2 (4½" × 22½") side outer borders.
- 8 (2½"-wide) strips. From strips, cut 300 (1" × 2½") A rectangles for blocks.

From yellow print, cut:

- 4 (2¼"-wide) strips for binding.
- 4 Pineapples.

From green solid, cut:

- 8 (1¼" × 11") bias strips for vines. Fold bias strips in thirds, press, and hand baste fold in place to prepare vines for appliqué.
- 68 Leaves.

From one blue print fat eighth, cut:

- 4 Baskets.

From remaining fat eighths, cut a total of:

- 300 (1" × 2½") A rectangles for blocks.
- 100 (1½" × 2½") B rectangles for blocks.
- 20 Berries.

Block Assembly

1. Trace Paper Piecing Pattern on page 38 onto tracing paper.
2. Choose 4 sets of 3 matching print A rectangles and 1 B rectangle, 12 cream A rectangles, and 1 yellow C square. Paper piece block in numerical order. Use C square for piece #1; use A rectangles for pieces #2–25; use B rectangles for pieces #26–29.
3. Make 25 Pineapple blocks.

Quilt Assembly

1. Referring to *Quilt Top Assembly Diagram*, lay out blocks as shown. Join into rows; join rows to complete quilt center.
2. Add yellow side inner borders to quilt center. Add yellow top and bottom inner borders to quilt. Repeat for cream outer borders.

Border Appliqué

1. Referring to photo on page 36, position vines, leaves, baskets, berries, and pineapples on outer border.

2. Appliqué pieces on quilt.

Finishing

1. Layer backing, batting, and quilt top; baste. Quilt as desired. Quilt shown was outline quilted around appliqué, has diagonal lines through each block, and has parallel diagonal lines in outer border *(Quilting Diagram)*.

2. Join 2¼"-wide yellow print strips into 1 continuous piece for straight-grain French-fold binding. Add binding to quilt.

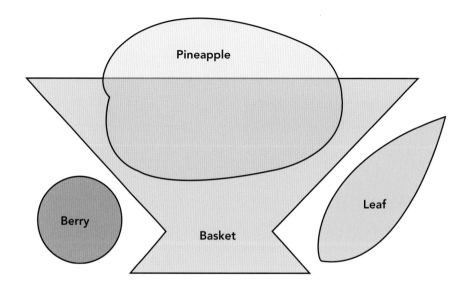

Quilting Diagram

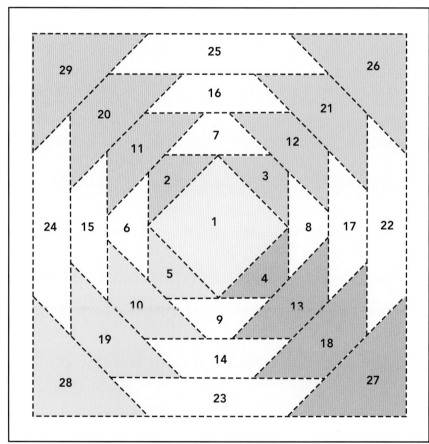

Paper Piecing Pattern

DESIGNER

An enthusiastic quilter from the start, Judy Flanagan began quilting in the mid-1970s. She loves traditional patterns and began designing her own quilts in the early 90s. Judy is the former owner of The Quilter's Coop quilt shop in Sanborn, Iowa, and is now enjoying retirement. ✳

Sew Easy™

Paper Foundation Piecing

Paper foundation piecing is ideal for small, intricate designs with odd angles and sizes of pieces.

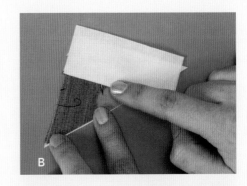

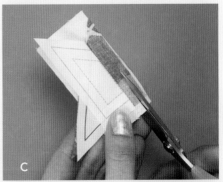

1. Using a ruler and pencil, trace the outline of all shapes and the outer edge of the foundation pattern onto tracing paper. Number the pieces to indicate the stitching order. Using fabric pieces that are larger that the numbered areas, place fabrics for #1 and #2 right sides together. Position paper pattern atop fabrics with printed side of paper facing you *(Photo A)*. Make sure the fabric for #1 is under that area and that edges of fabrics extend ¼" beyond stitching line between the two sections.

2. Using a short machine stitch so papers will tear off easily later, sew on stitching line between the two areas, extending stitching into seam allowances at ends of seams.

3. Open out pieces and press or finger press the seam *(Photo B)*. The right sides will be facing out on the back side of the paper patttern.

4. Flip the work over and fold back paper pattern on sewn line. Trim seam allowance to ¼", being careful not to cut paper pattern *(Photo C)*.

5. Continue to add pieces in numerical order until pattern is covered. Use rotary cutter and ruler to trim excess paper and fabric along outer pattern lines *(Photo D)*.

6. Join pieced sections to complete block *(Photo E)*.

7. Carefully tear off foundation paper.

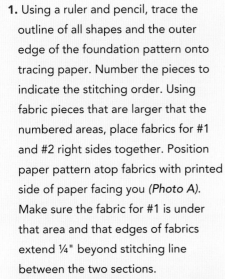

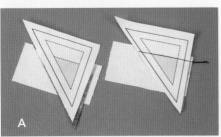

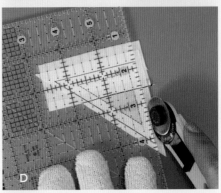

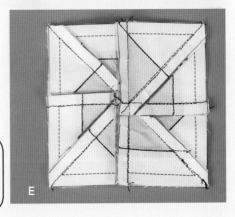

Sew Smart™

Instead of tracing paper, try one of the new water-soluble paper products. Instead of tearing off the paper after sewing, just moisten, and the paper disappears! —Liz

Weathervane

Use Penny Haren's Pieced Appliqué™ technique to create blocks that look pieced to perfection! *See Sew Easy: Pieced Appliqué™ on page 43 for detailed instructions.*

PROJECT RATING: EASY
Size: 15" × 35"
Blocks: 10 (6") Weathervane blocks

MATERIALS

1¼ yards white print for blocks and sashing squares
¾ yard black print for blocks and binding
½ yard green solid for blocks
⅜ yard pink solid for sashing
½ yard backing fabric
Water-soluble glue stick
Paper
Permanent pen
Freezer paper
Craft-size quilt batting

Cutting

Measurements include ¼" seam allowances. Patterns for Square and Triangle are on page 42. Follow instructions in *Sew Easy: Pieced Appliqué* on page 43 to make paper templates and cut Squares and Triangles.

From white print fabric, cut:

- 18 (1½") sashing squares.
- 40 Squares.
- 80 Triangles.

Sew **Smart**™

Fussy cutting the squares and triangles will add drama to this block. —Penny

From black print fabric, cut:

- 5 (2½"-wide) strips for strip sets.
- 3 (2¼"-wide) strips for binding.

From green solid fabric, cut:

- 4 (2½"-wide) strips for strip sets.

From pink solid fabric, cut:

- 5 (1½"-wide) strips. From strips, cut 27 (1½" × 6½") sashing rectangles.

Block Foundation Assembly

1. Join 2 black print strips and 1 green solid strip as shown in *Strip Set #1 Diagram* on page 42. Make 2 Strip Set #1. From strip sets, cut 20 (2½"-wide) #1 segments.

Sew Smart™

When making strip sets and assembling block foundations, press seam allowances open to reduce bulk. —Liz

2½"

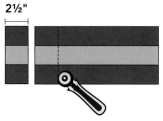

Strip Set #1 Diagram

2. In the same manner, join 2 green solid strips and 1 black print strip as shown in *Strip Set #2 Diagram*. From strip set, cut 10 (2½"-wide) #2 segments.

2½"

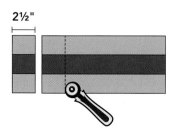

Strip Set #2 Diagram

3. Referring to *Block Foundation Diagrams*, join 2 #1 segments and 1 #2 segment to make 1 Block Foundation.

#1 #2 #1

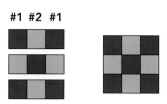

Block Foundation Diagrams
Make 10 block foundations.

Block Assembly

1. Prepare and stitch appliqué pieces to block foundation following instructions in *Sew Easy: Pieced Appliqué* on page 43. Remove paper templates and press block.

2. Make 10 Weathervane blocks.

Quilt Assembly

1. Lay out blocks, sashing rectangles, and sashing squares as shown in *Quilt Top Assembly Diagram*.

2. Join into rows, join rows to complete quilt top.

Quilt Top Assembly Diagram

Finishing

1. Layer backing, batting, and quilt top; baste. Quilt as desired. Quilt shown was quilted with a flower design in each block and straight lines in sashing *(Quilting Diagram)*.

2. Join 2¼"-wide black print strips into 1 continuous piece for straight-grain French-fold binding. Add binding to quilt.

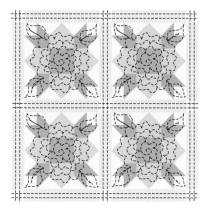

Quilting Diagram

Square

Triangle

For more than twenty years, Penny Haren has been developing and teaching techniques that make quilting easy and fun. She also designed new rulers with Creative Grids® that are perfect complements to her Pieced Appliqué™ method. Her books, *Penny Haren's Pieced Appliqué* and *Penny Haren's Pieced Appliqué: More Blocks & Projects*, are published by Landauer Corporation. ✳

Sew Easy™
Pieced Appliqué™

Use this method to make Weathervane blocks with no inset pieces.
You see exactly what your finished block will look like before anything is stitched,
enabling you to fussy cut details in blocks. If you like to hand appliqué, you can
carry blocks with you to work on wherever you go.

1. Following instructions on page 42, make block foundation.

2. Copy or trace Square pattern on regular typing paper.

3. Fuse freezer paper to wrong side (unprinted side) of copied or traced pattern. Trim on the line to make template.

Sew Smart™
Use a "paper blade" in your rotary cutter when trimming templates. —Liz

4. Glue Square template to wrong side of white print fabric. Trim fabric ¼" away from template on all sides (Photo A).

5. Turn under seam allowances on 2 adjoining sides of template; glue to template.

6. Place appliqué pieces atop the block foundation, aligning raw edges of appliqué pieces and block foundation (Photos B, C, and D).

7. Using matching thread, hand stitch the turned edges of the appliqué pieces to the foundation using an invisible appliqué stitch. Leave the raw edges open. If you prefer, machine appliqué using a narrow zigzag stitch and invisible thread.

Sew Smart™
Stitch all squares in place before placing triangles atop block foundation. —Marianne

8. When all stitching is done, place block into warm water to dissolve glue. Remove block and roll in a towel to remove excess water. Pull out paper templates.

9. Press block on terry towel. Press on wrong side to make sure all seams are pressed correctly.

Sew Smart™
Use spray starch when pressing to give block a crisp look. —Penny

Garden Gathering

Large prints of poppies and hydrangeas team up with bright solids in this
great little quilt for the wall or table top. Embellish with silk ribbon embroidery for a special touch.

PROJECT RATING: INTERMEDIATE
Size: 45½" × 45½"

MATERIALS

1½ yards large poppy print

⅞ yard medium floral print

1¼ yards black dot

4 fat quarters★ assorted solids in
orange, green, tan, and pink

3 yards backing fabric

16½" square template plastic

Silk embroidery ribbon (4mm and
7mm) in assorted colors to match
fabric

Fons & Porter Flying Geese Ruler
(optional)

Twin-size quilt batting

★fat quarter = 18" × 20"

Cutting

Measurements include ¼" seam
allowances.

NOTE: To cut both kinds of triangles
(A and B) from the same size strips,
using the Fons & Porter Flying Geese
Ruler, see *Sew Easy: Making Flying*

Geese Units on page 47. If you are
not using the Fons & Porter Flying
Geese Ruler, use the cutting NOTE
instructions given here.

From large poppy print, cut:

• 1 (16½") square for quilt center. Lay
template plastic square atop fabric,
centering design. Draw around square;
cut with scissors or rotary cutter on
drawn line.

> ### Sew **Smart**™
> Center square of quilt will be placed
> on point. Pay attention to direction
> of poppies when cutting square. —
> Marianne

• 2 (11⅞"-wide) strips. From strips, cut
4 (11⅞") D squares.

From medium floral print, cut:

• 2 (12¼"-wide) strips. From strips, cut
4 (12¼") squares. Cut squares in half
diagonally to make 8 half-square C
triangles.

From black dot, cut:

• 1 (8½"-wide) strip. From strip, cut
2 (8½") E squares.

• 3 (4½"-wide) strips. From strips, cut

2 quarter-square B triangles and
32 half-square A triangles.

NOTE: If not using the Fons & Porter
Flying Geese Ruler, cut

• 1 (9¼"-wide) strip. From strip, cut 1
(9¼") square. Cut square in half
diagonally in both directions to
make 4 quarter-square B triangles
(2 are extra).

• 2 (4⅞"-wide) strips. From strip, cut
16 (4⅞") squares. Cut squares in half
diagonally to make 32 half-square A
triangles.

• 5 (2¼"-wide) strips for binding.

From each solid fat quarter, cut:

• 3 (4½"-wide) strips. From strips, cut
6 quarter-square B triangles.

NOTE: If not using the Fons & Porter
Flying Geese Ruler, cut

• 1 (9¼"-wide) strip. From strip, cut
2 (9¼") squares. Cut squares in half
diagonally in both directions to
make 8 quarter-square B triangles
(you will have a few extra).

Block Assembly

1. Join 2 black dot A triangles and 1
pink B triangle as shown in *Flying*

Geese Unit Diagrams. Make 4 pink Flying Geese Units.

2. In the same manner, make 4 tan, 4 orange, and 4 green Flying Geese Units.

3. Referring to *Quilt Top Assembly Diagram,* join 4 matching Flying Geese Units to make 1 Flying Geese Section. Repeat to make 4 Flying Geese Sections.

4. Join 1 black dot B triangle, 2 orange B triangles, and 1 green B triangle as shown in *Hourglass Unit Diagrams.*

5. In the same manner, make 1 Hourglass Unit using 1 black dot, 1 pink, and 2 tan B triangles.

Quilt Assembly

1. Referring to *Quilt Top Assembly Diagram,* lay out center square, Flying Geese Sections, and Hourglass Units. Join into diagonal rows; join rows to make complete center.

2. Referring to *Quilt Top Assembly Diagram,* join 2 medium floral C triangles and 1 large Poppy D square to make 1 Corner Unit. Make 4 Corner Units.

3. Add Corner Units to quilt center.

Finishing

1. Divide backing fabric into 2 (1½-yard) lengths. Cut 1 piece in half lengthwise to make 2 narrow panels. Join 1 narrow panel to wider panel. Remaining panel is extra and can be used to make a hanging sleeve.

2. Layer backing, batting, and quilt top; baste. Quilt shown was outline quilted around each flower petal and has an allover freehand feather design in the Flying Geese Sections and Corner Units *(Quilting Diagram).*

Flying Geese Unit Diagrams

Hourglass Unit Diagrams

Quilt Top Assembly Diagram

3. Join 2¼"-wide black dot strips into 1 continuous piece for straight-grain French-fold binding. Add binding to quilt.

4. Using silk embroidery ribbon, make French Knots in the centers of flowers, mixing colors as desired *(French Knot Diagram).*

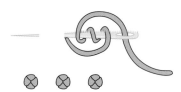

French Knot Diagram

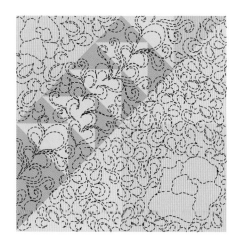

Quilting Diagram

DESIGNER

Laura Heine's fabric collections abound with bold, large-scale designs based on her watercolor art. She is an award-winning quilt artist who transforms colorful threads, embellishments, fusible appliqué, and piecework into amazing quilts. Laura teaches nationally, encouraging students to express themselves in their quilts. ✳

Sew Easy™

Making Flying Geese Units

The Fons & Porter Flying Geese Ruler takes the guesswork out of cutting the triangles for Flying Geese Units in finished sizes from 1" × 2" to 4" × 8". Both the large "goose" triangle and the smaller "sky" triangles are cut from the same width strips.

1. To cut the large "goose" triangle, select black line on ruler that corresponds to the desired finished size Flying Geese Unit. (For the Flying Geese Units in *Garden Gathering* on page 44, the finished size is 4" × 8". For the Flying Geese Units in *Chained Stars* on page 98, the finished size is 2" × 4".)

2. Follow across black line to right edge of ruler and cut a fabric strip the width indicted. For example, to cut the large triangle for the 4" × 8" finished-size Flying Geese Unit, cut a 4½"-wide fabric strip. To cut the large triangle for the 2" × 4" finished-size Flying Geese Unit, cut a 2½"-wide fabric strip.

3. Cut "goose" triangles as shown in *Photo A*, first placing the black cutting guideline along bottom cut edge of strip and then along top edge of strip.

4. To cut the corresponding smaller "sky" triangles, select the yellow line that corresponds to the desired finished size Flying Geese Unit.

5. Follow across yellow line to left edge of ruler and cut a fabric strip the width

indicated. For example, to cut the small triangles for a 4" × 8" finished-size Flying Geese Unit, cut a 4½"-wide fabric strip. To cut the small triangle for the 2" × 4" finished-size Flying Geese Unit, cut a 2½"-wide fabric strip.

6. Cut triangles as shown, first placing the yellow cutting guideline along bottom edge of strip and then along top edge (*Photo B*). The yellow shaded area of the ruler will extend beyond the edge of the strip.

7. Join "sky" triangles to center "goose" triangle to complete 1 Flying Geese Unit (*Photo C*).

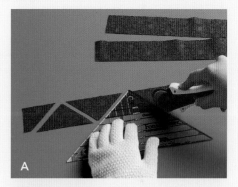

A

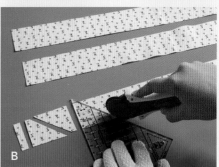

B

Sew Smart™

Your half-square triangles will be pre-trimmed with the tiny fabric tips that you usually cut off after sewing already eliminated. Cut these triangles with strip folded in half so that half of the triangles are trimmed on the right end and the other half of them on the left end (*Photo C*). —Marianne

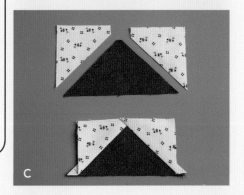

C

Summer

PROJECT BY **Alison Ripperger and Sharon Hart**.

Nine Patch Picnic

Love of Quilting staffers Alison Ripperger and Sharon Hart made this quick quilt in fruit and veggie prints to use as a picnic throw. The design by Nancy Tacchi Derr first ran as a flannel quilt in the November/December 2000 issue of *Love of Quilting*.

PROJECT RATING: EASY
Size: 50" × 50"
Blocks: 16 (10") Crazy Nine Patch blocks

MATERIALS

18 fat quarters★ assorted fruit and vegetable prints for blocks and outer border
⅜ yard red print for inner border
12" or larger rotary cutting square
3 yards backing fabric
Twin-size quilt batting
★fat quarter = 18" × 20"

Cutting

Measurements include ¼" seam allowances. Border strips are exact length needed. You may want to make them longer to allow for piecing variations.

From each fat quarter, cut:

• 1 (12") square for blocks.
• 1 (4"-wide) strip for outer border.

From remainder of 1 fat quarter, cut:

• 4 (2") squares for inner border corners.

From red print, cut:

• 4 (2"-wide) strips. From strips, cut 4 (2" × 40½") inner borders.

Block Assembly

1. Stack 9 fruit/vegetable print squares, aligning all edges. Using rotary cutter and ruler, make 1 diagonal cut through stack at least 1" from edge as shown in *Diagram 1*.

2. Take top small piece and put on bottom of stack.

3. Join 2 top pieces from stack *(Diagram 2)*. Continue chain piecing all pairs of pieces in stack.

4. Cut chain threads and press seam allowances toward smaller pieces. Restack blocks in original order.

5. Make cut #2 at least 1" away from edge as shown in *Diagram 3*.

6. Put the top *two* small pieces at the bottom of the stack. Chain piece, press seams toward smaller pieces, and restack blocks in original order.

7. Turn stack 90 degrees and make cut #3. Place the top *three* smaller pieces at bottom of the stack and join as shown in *Diagram 4*.

8. Make cut #4. Place top *six* smaller pieces at the bottom of the stack and join as shown in *Diagram 5*.

9. You will have 9 Crazy Nine Patch blocks, each made of 9 fabrics in 9 different shapes. Trim blocks to 10½" with rotary cutting square.

10. Repeat steps #1–#9 to make 9 additional Crazy Nine Patch blocks. (You will have 2 extra.)

Quilt Assembly

1. Referring to *Quilt Top Assembly Diagram*, lay out blocks in 4 horizontal rows with 4 blocks in each row, rotating blocks as desired.

2. Join blocks into rows; join rows to complete quilt center.

3. Add red print side inner borders to quilt center. Add 1 (2") square to each end of remaining borders. Add borders to top and bottom of quilt.

4. Cut 4"-wide fruit/vegetable print strips into random-length pieces. Join pieces to make 2 (4" × 43½") side outer borders and 2 (4" × 50½") top and bottom outer borders. Add side borders to quilt center. Add top and bottom borders to quilt.

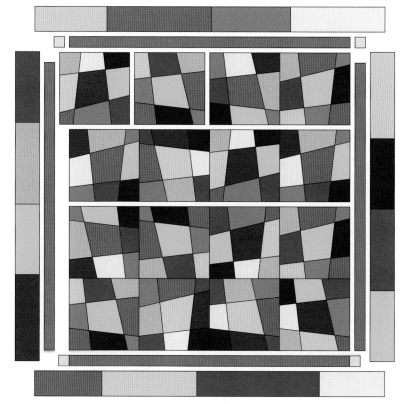

Quilt Top Assembly Diagram

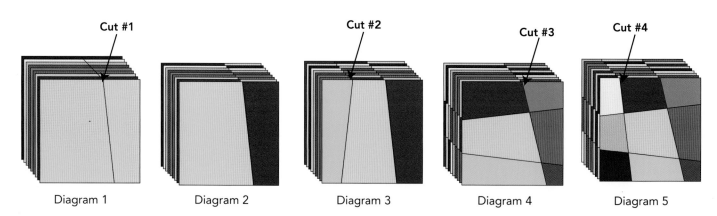

| Diagram 1 | Diagram 2 | Diagram 3 | Diagram 4 | Diagram 5 |

Cut #1 — Cut #2 — Cut #3 — Cut #4

Finishing

1. Divide backing into 2 (1½-yard) pieces. Cut 1 piece in half lengthwise. Sew 1 narrow panel to wider panel. Press seam allowances toward narrow panel. Remaining panel is extra and can be used to make a hanging sleeve.

2. Layer backing and quilt top, right sides together. Stitch around quilt top ¼" from outer edge, leaving an 8" opening for turning. Turn quilt right side out and whipstitch opening closed.

TRIED & TRUE

Retail manager Sharon Hart used 1930s reproduction prints for her quilt.

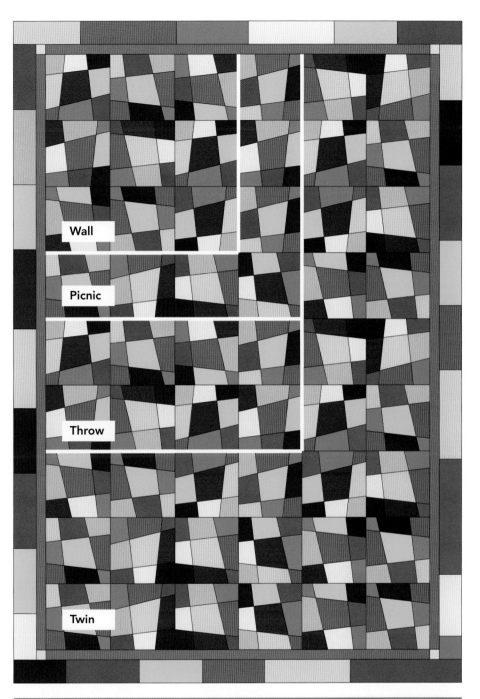

Wall

Picnic

Throw

Twin

ALTERNATE SIZE CHART

	Wall Quilt	Throw	Twin
Finished size	40" × 40"	50" × 70"	70" × 100"
Layout	3 × 3	4 × 6	6 × 9
Fat quarters for blocks	9	27	54
Inner border fabric	¼ yard	⅜ yard	⅝ yard

Country Garden

Simple pieced blocks form the perfect background for folk art flowers in this country-fresh table topper by Deanne Eisenman.

Size: 28" × 28"
Blocks: 4 (8") Chain blocks

MATERIALS

⅞ yard tan print for blocks
¼ yard light tan print for border
⅜ yard dark blue print for border
¼ yard red print for blocks
⅜ yard dark red print for binding
1 fat quarter★★ green print for
    stems and leaves
6 fat eighths★ light green, purple,
    brown, gold, dark red, and dark
    blue prints for appliqué
Paper-backed fusible web
1 yard backing fabric
Craft-size quilt batting
★fat eighth = 9" × 20"
★★fat quarter = 18" × 20"

Cutting

Measurements include ¼" seam allowances. Patterns for appliqué pieces are on pages 57–59. Follow manufacturer's instructions for using fusible web.

From tan print, cut:
• 2 (8½"-wide) strips. From strips, cut
  5 (8½") C squares.
• 1 (2½"-wide) strip. From strip, cut
  16 (2½") A squares.
• 5 (1½"-wide) strips. From 3 strips, cut
  16 (1½" × 6½") D rectangles.
  Remaining strips are for strip sets.

From light tan print, cut:
• 3 (2½"-wide) strips. From strips, cut
  24 (2½" × 4½") E rectangles.

From dark blue print, cut:
• 4 (2½"-wide) strips. From strips, cut
  56 (2½") A squares.

From red print, cut:
• 3 (1½"-wide) strips. From 1 strip, cut
  16 (1½") B squares. Remaining strips
  are for strip sets.

From dark red print, cut:
• 4 (2¼"-wide) strips for binding.

From green fat quarter, cut:
• 65" of (1⅛"-wide) bias strips for
  stems. Fold strips in thirds, press,
  and hand baste folds in place to
  prepare stems for appliqué. Cut
  4 (7¼"-long) stems and 8 (4¼"-long)
  stems.
• 16 Leaves.

From light green fat eighth, cut:
• 4 Flower Calyxes.
• 1 Center Medallion #5.

From purple fat eighth, cut:
• 4 Flowers.

From brown fat eighth, cut:
• 4 Flower Centers.

From gold fat eighth, cut:
• 1 Center Medallion #2.

From dark red fat eighth, cut:
• 8 Flower Buds.
• 1 Center Medallion #3.

From dark blue fat eighth, cut:
• 8 Flower Bud Centers.
• 1 Center Medallion #4.
• 1 Center Medallion #1.

Background Assembly

1. Join 1 tan print strip and 1 red print
   strip as shown in *Strip Set Diagram*.
   Make 2 strip sets. From strip sets, cut
   32 (1½") segments.

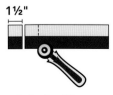

Strip Set Diagram

2. Join 2 strip set segments to make 1 Four Patch Unit *(Four Patch Unit Diagrams)*. Make 16 Four Patch Units.

Four Patch Unit Diagrams

3. Lay out 4 tan print A squares, 1 dark blue print A square, 4 Four Patch Units, 4 tan print D rectangles, and 4 red print B squares as shown in *Block Assembly Diagram*. Join to complete 1 Chain block *(Block Diagram)*. Make 4 blocks.

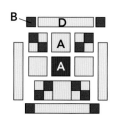

Block Assembly Diagram

Block Diagram

4. Lay out blocks and tan print C squares as shown in *Background Assembly Diagram*. Join into rows, join rows to complete background *(Background Diagram)*.

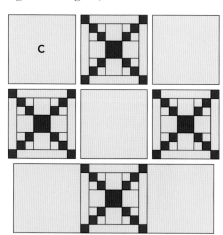

Background Assembly Diagram

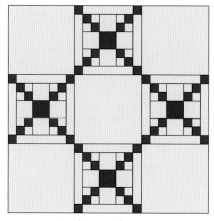

Background Diagram

Border Assembly

1. Referring to *Flying Geese Unit Diagrams*, place 1 dark blue print A square atop 1 light tan E rectangle, right sides facing. Stitch diagonally from corner to corner as shown. Trim ¼" beyond stitching. Press open to reveal triangle. Repeat for opposite corner to complete 1 Flying Geese Unit. Make 24 Flying Geese Units.

Flying Geese Unit Diagrams

2. Referring to *Quilt Top Assembly Diagram*, join 6 Flying Geese Units as shown to make 1 pieced border. Make 4 pieced borders.

Quilt Assembly

1. Add pieced borders to sides of background as shown in *Quilt Top Assembly Diagram*.

2. Add 1 dark blue print A square to each end of remaining pieced borders. Add borders to top and bottom of background.

Quilt Top Assembly Diagram

3. Referring to photo on page 55 for placement, position stems and appliqué pieces on pieced background. Appliqué pieces in place.

Finishing

1. Layer backing, batting, and quilt top; baste. Quilt as desired. Quilt shown was outline quilted around appliqué pieces and has allover meandering with stars in the background and borders *(Quilting Diagram)*.

2. Join 2¼"-wide dark red print strips into 1 continuous piece for straight-grain French fold binding. Add binding to quilt.

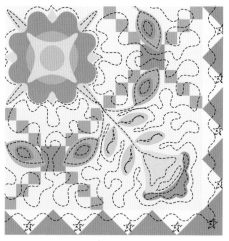

Quilting Diagram

Patterns are shown full size for use with fusible web. Add ³⁄₁₆" seam allowance for hand appliqué.

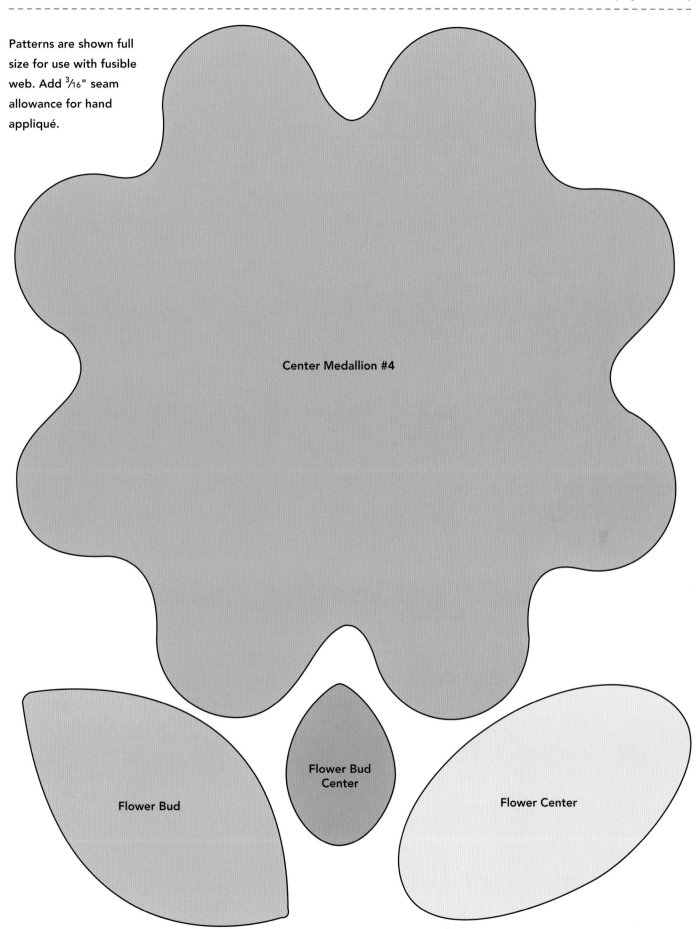

Center Medallion #4

Flower Bud

Flower Bud Center

Flower Center

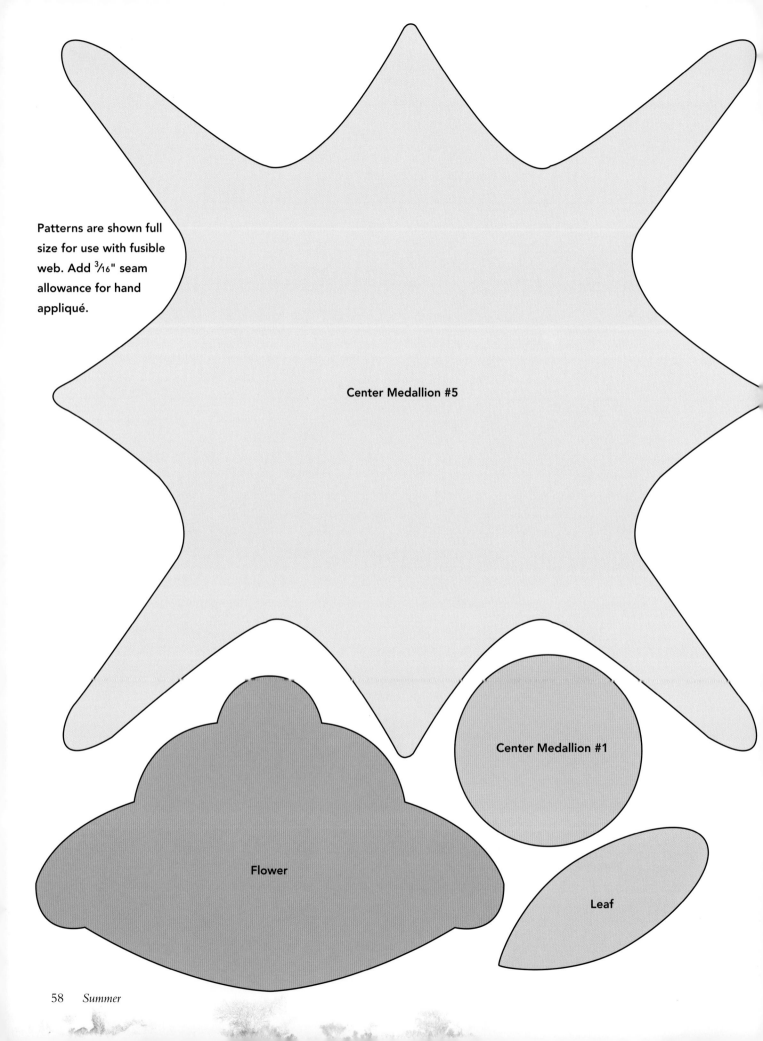

Patterns are shown full size for use with fusible web. Add $^3/_{16}$" seam allowance for hand appliqué.

Center Medallion #5

Center Medallion #1

Flower

Leaf

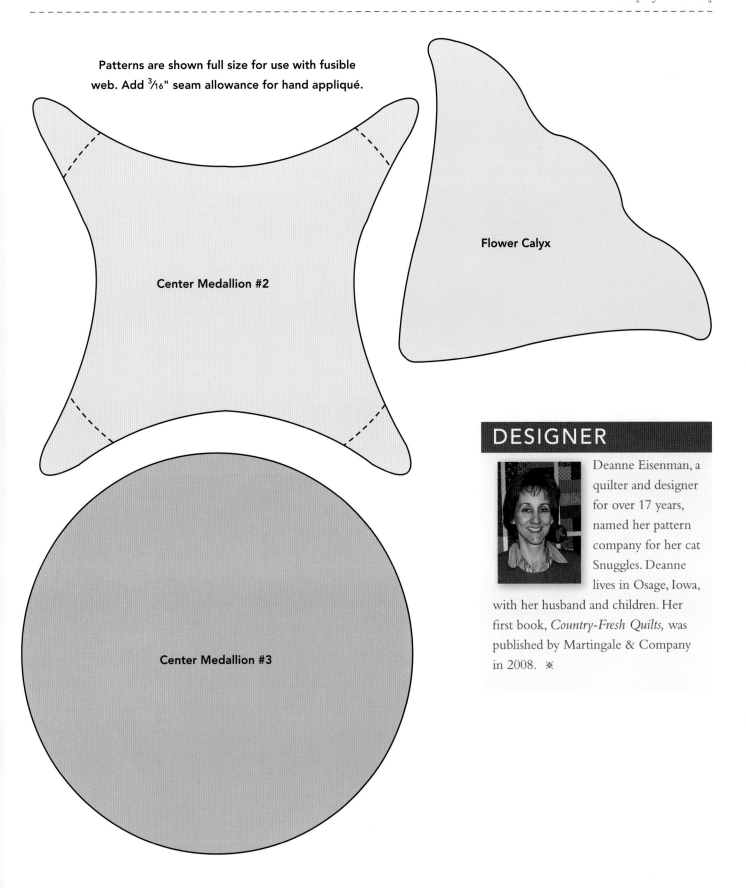

Patterns are shown full size for use with fusible web. Add 3/16" seam allowance for hand appliqué.

Flower Calyx

Center Medallion #2

Center Medallion #3

DESIGNER

Deanne Eisenman, a quilter and designer for over 17 years, named her pattern company for her cat Snuggles. Deanne lives in Osage, Iowa, with her husband and children. Her first book, *Country-Fresh Quilts,* was published by Martingale & Company in 2008. ✳

PROJECT BY **Rachel Wells**.
MACHINE QUILTED BY **Cynthia Spethman**.

Birthday Stars

Make this bright quilt with our freezer paper technique to create unique stars without using templates. *See Sew Easy: Making Stars* on page 65. Cutting instructions for a table runner size are on page 64.

PROJECT RATING: INTERMEDIATE

Size: 49" × 57"

Blocks: 18 (8") Star blocks
2 (8") Four Patch blocks

MATERIALS

18 fat quarters★★ assorted bright prints for large Star blocks and pieced outer border

4 fat eighths★ assorted bright prints for small Star blocks

⅜ yard green plaid for inner border

1 yard orange print for middle border and binding

Freezer paper

3½ yards backing fabric

Twin-size quilt batting

★fat eighth = 9" × 20"

★★fat quarter = 18" × 20"

Cutting

Measurements include ¼" seam allowances. Border strips are exact length needed. You may want to make them longer to allow for piecing variations.

From each fat quarter, cut:
- 2 (2½"-wide) strips. From strips, cut 6 (2½" × 5½") rectangles.
- 1 (12") A square.

From each fat eighth, cut:
- 1 (8") B square.
- 1 (4½") C square.

From green plaid, cut:
- 5 (1¾"-wide) strips. Piece 3 strips to make 2 (1¾" × 40½") side inner borders. From remaining strips, cut 2 (1¾" × 35") top and bottom inner borders.

From orange print, cut:
- 5 (2¾"-wide) strips. Piece 3 strips to make 2 (2¾" × 43") side middle borders. From remaining strips, cut 2 (2¾" × 39½") top and bottom middle borders.
- 6 (2¼"-wide) strips for binding.

Quilt Top Assembly Diagram

Star Block Assembly

1. Make 18 large Star blocks as described in *Sew Easy: Making Stars* on page 65, using 18 print A squares and 8" squares of freezer paper.

2. In the same manner, make 4 small Star blocks using 4 print B squares and 4" squares of freezer paper.

Four Patch Block Assembly

1. Lay out 2 small Star blocks and 2 C squares, as shown in *Four Patch Assembly Diagram*. Join into rows; join rows to complete 1 Four Patch block *(Block Diagram)*. Make 2 Four Patch blocks.

Pieced Border Assembly

1. Referring to *Quilt Top Assembly Diagram*, join 26 rectangles to make 1 side border. Repeat for other side border.

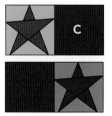

Four Patch
Assembly Diagram

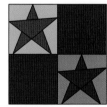

Four Patch
Block Diagram

2. In the same manner, join 22 border rectangles to make top border. Repeat for bottom border.

Quilt Assembly

1. Lay out Star blocks and Four Patch blocks as shown in *Quilt Top Assembly Diagram*.

2. Join into rows; join rows to complete quilt center.

3. Add green plaid side inner borders to quilt center. Add top and bottom inner borders to quilt. Repeat for orange print middle borders.

4. Add one side border to right edge of quilt, starting at top and stopping 1" before edge of orange print border.

5. Add top border to quilt. Add left side border to quilt. Add bottom border to quilt, keeping right side border out of the way.

6. Finish stitching right side border seam.

Finishing

1. Divide backing fabric into 2 (1¾-yard) lengths. Cut 1 piece in half lengthwise to make 2 narrow panels. Join 1 narrow panel to wider panel; press seam allowances toward narrow panel. Remaining panel is extra and can be used to make a hanging sleeve.

2. Layer backing, batting, and quilt top; baste. Quilt as desired. Quilt shown was outline quilted around stars, has an overall star and loop design in the orange and green borders, and has a spiral design in the star backgrounds *(Quilting Diagram)*.

3. Join 2¼"-wide orange print strips into 1 continuous piece for straight-grain French-fold binding. Add binding to quilt.

Quilting Diagram

TRIED & TRUE

Enhance your summer celebrations with a festive table runner. Fabrics used are from the Democracy collection by Sandy Gervais for Moda.

Size: 20" × 44"

Blocks: 3 (8") Star blocks

8 (4") Star blocks

MATERIALS

¾ yard blue print

½ yard red print

⅜ yard tan print

½ yard beige print

⅜ yard binding fabric

Freezer paper

1⅜ yards backing fabric

24" × 48" piece quilt batting

Cutting

Measurements include ¼" seam allowances.

From blue print, cut:

• 2 (2½" × 40½") top and bottom borders.

• 2 (2½" × 20½") side borders.

• 3 (12") squares.

From red print, cut:

• 4 (8") squares.

• 20 (2½" × 4½") rectangles.

From tan print, cut:

• 3 (12") squares.

From beige print, cut:

• 4 (8") squares.

• 20 (2½" × 4½") rectangles.

From binding fabric, cut:

• 4 (2¼"-wide) strips.

DESIGNER

Rachel Wells has been quilting for over twenty years. She likes to work on several fun projects while mulling over a more challenging one. Rachel lives in Missoula, Montana. ✳

Sew Easy™
Making Stars

Make one-of-a-kind stars using our freezer paper pattern technique. Changing the placement of the pattern marks makes each block unique.

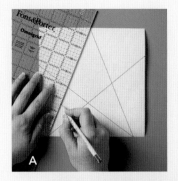

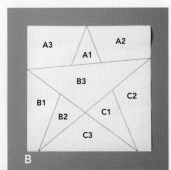

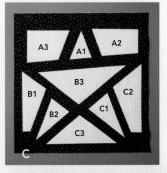

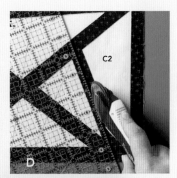

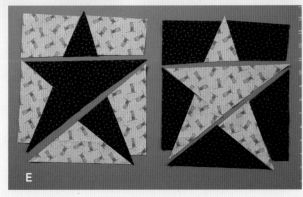

Sew Smart™
Read through all instructions before starting. —Marianne

1. Make a mark near center of top edge of 8″ freezer paper square. Make a mark on left edge and one on right edge at least 2″ from top corners of paper. Make 2 marks on bottom edge at least 1″ from each corner.
Note: Measurements are not exact. Moving the marks changes the shape of star, making each unique.

2. Using a ruler and pencil, connect marks as shown in *Photo A*. Erase 2 lines in center section. Label each section as shown in *Photo B*.

3. Cut sections apart on drawn lines.

4. Stack 1 dark 12″ square atop 1 light 12″ square, right sides up. Press freezer paper pieces on top square in order as shown in *Photo C*, leaving at least ½″ between pieces. Place ¼″ line of ruler on edge of paper pattern and cut out each shape *(Photo D)*.

5. Remove freezer paper. Lay out pieces as shown in *Photo E*. You will have pieces for one block with a dark star and light background and one block with a light star and dark background. Piece section A in numerical order using ¼″ seams. Repeat for sections B and C.

6. Join sections to complete 2 Star blocks *(Photo F)*. If necessary, trim to 8½″ square.

Sew Smart™
To make 4″-finished Star blocks, begin with a 4″ square of freezer paper and 8″ squares of fabric. —Liz

Puzzled

Quiltmaker Wanda Ingram added excitement to these traditional Churn Dash blocks by altering the sashing strips so that light-colored Churn Dash blocks appear between the colored blocks.

PROJECT RATING: INTERMEDIATE
Size: 34" × 34"
Blocks: 9 (6") Churn Dash blocks

MATERIALS

5 fat eighths★ red prints
5 fat eighths★ assorted blue prints
5 fat eighths★ light prints
½ yard blue print for borders
1 yard red print for borders and
  binding
1⅛ yards backing fabric
Crib-size quilt batting
★fat eighth = 9" × 20"

Cutting

Measurements include ¼" seam allowances. Border strips are exact length needed. You may want to make them longer to allow for piecing variations.

From each red print fat eighth, cut:

- 1 (2⅞"-wide) strip. From strip cut 2 (2⅞") squares. Cut squares in half diagonally to make 4 half-square A triangles.
- 1 (2½"-wide) strip. From strip cut 1 (2½" × 4½") D rectangle, 1 (2½") B square, and 2 (2½" × 1½") C rectangles. You will have extra pieces.
- 1 (1½" × 11") strip for strip sets.

From each blue print fat eighth, cut:

- 1 (2⅞"-wide) strip. From strip cut 2 (2⅞") squares. Cut squares in half diagonally to make 4 half-square A triangles.
- 1 (2½"-wide) strip. From strip cut 1 (2½" × 4½") D rectangle, 1 (2½") B square, and 2 (2½" × 1½") C rectangles. You will have extra pieces.
- 1 (1½" × 11") strip for strip sets.

From each light print fat eighth, cut:

- 1 (2⅞"-wide) strip. From strip cut 4 (2⅞") squares. Cut squares in half diagonally to make 8 half-square A triangles.
- 1 (2½"-wide) strip. From strip cut 1 (2½" × 4½") D rectangle, 2 (2½") B squares, and 4 (2½" × 1½") C rectangles. You will have extra pieces.
- 2 (1½" × 11") strips for strip sets.

From blue print, cut:

- 6 (2½"-wide) strips. From strips, cut 2 (2½" × 22½") side inner borders,

2 (2½" × 26½") top and bottom inner borders, 3 (2½" × 20") strips, and 4 (2½") B squares.

From red print, cut:

- 6 (2½"-wide) strips. From strips, cut 2 (2½" × 30½") side outer borders, 2 (2½" × 34½") top and bottom outer borders, 3 (2½" × 20") strips, and 4 (2½") B squares.
- 4 (2¼"-wide) strips for binding.

Block Assembly

1. Choose 4 matching light print A triangles, 4 matching blue print A triangles, 1 light print strip, 1 red print strip, and 1 matching light print B square.

2. Join 1 light print A triangle and 1 blue print A triangle as shown in *Triangle-Square Diagrams*. Make 4 triangle-squares.

Triangle-Square Diagrams

3. Join 1 light print strip and 1 red print strip as shown in *Strip Set #1 Diagram*. From strip set, cut 4 (2½"-wide) side units.

Strip Set #1 Diagram

4. Lay out triangle-squares, side units, and light print B square as shown in *Block Assembly Diagram*. Join into rows; join rows to complete 1 Churn Dash block *(Block Diagram)*.

Block Assembly Diagram   Block Diagram

5. Referring to photo on page 66 and *Quilt Top Assembly Diagram* for color placement, make 8 additional Churn Dash blocks.

Sashing Assembly

1. Join 1 light print C rectangle, 1 blue print C rectangle, and 1 red print D rectangle as shown in *Outer Sashing Unit Diagrams*. Make 4 red outer sashing units. In the same manner, make 4 blue outer sashing units using 1 light print C rectangle, 1 red print C rectangle, and 1 blue print D rectangle in each.

Outer Sashing Unit Diagrams

2. Join 2 light print C rectangles, 2 red print C rectangles, and 1 blue print B square as shown in *Inner Sashing Unit Diagrams*. Make 2 blue inner sashing units. In the same manner, make 2 red inner sashing units using 2 light print C rectangles, 2 blue print C rectangles, and 1 red print B square in each.

Inner Sashing Unit Diagrams

Quilt Assembly

1. Lay out blocks, B squares, and sashing units as shown in *Quilt Top Assembly Diagram*. Join into rows; join rows to complete quilt center.

2. Add blue print side inner borders to quilt center. Add blue print top and bottom inner borders to quilt.

3. Join 3 blue print and 3 red print strips as shown in *Strip Set #2 Diagram*.

4. From strip set, cut 8 (2½"-wide) segments. Join 2 segments to make 1 border strip. Make 4 border strips.

5. Add 1 blue print B square to each of 2 border strips to make side middle borders. Add to sides of quilt.

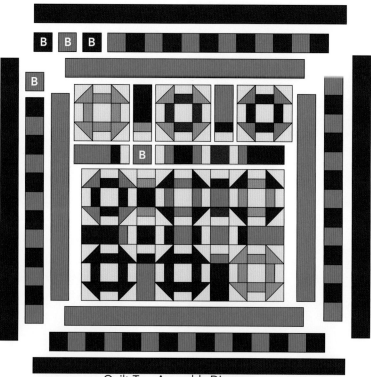

Quilt Top Assembly Diagram

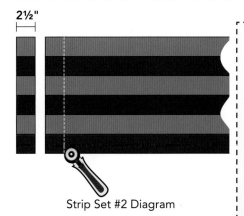

2½"

Strip Set #2 Diagram

6. Add 2 red print and 1 blue print B square as shown to each remaining border strip. Add to top and bottom of quilt center.

7. Add red print side outer borders to quilt. Add red print top and bottom outer borders to quilt.

Finishing

1. Layer backing, batting, and quilt top; baste. Quilt as desired.

2. Join 2¼"-wide red print strips into 1 continuous piece for straight-grain French-fold binding. Add binding to quilt.

DESIGNER

Wanda Bennett Ingram of Cartersville, Georgia, has been quilting for many years. "Before quilting, I tried several other crafts," says Wanda, "but I never enjoyed any of them. As soon as I made my first quilt, I realized that I had found my niche. I like all types of quilts, but I like traditional patterns best of all." ✳

Pieced Quilt Back

Wanda pieced a 30" Churn Dash framed with borders for her quilt back. Here are the materials list and instructions to make a pieced back for your quilt.

MATERIALS

1¼ yards light print
⅜ yard blue print
⅜ yard red print

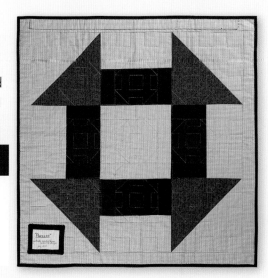

Cutting

From light print, cut:
- 1 (10⅞"-wide) strip. From strip, cut 2 (10⅞") squares and 1 (10½") B square for center. Cut 10⅞" squares in half diagonally to make 4 A half-square triangles for corner units.
- 2 (5½"-wide) strips. From strips, cut 4 (5½" × 10½") C rectangles for side units.
- 4 (4½"-wide) strips. From strips, cut 2 (4½" × 30½") side borders and 2 (4½" × 38½") top and bottom borders.

From blue print, cut:
- 1 (10⅞"-wide) strip. From strip, cut 2 (10⅞") squares. Cut squares in half diagonally to make 4 A half-square triangles for corner units.

From red print, cut:
- 2 (5½"-wide) strips. From strips, cut 4 (5½" × 10½") C rectangles for side units.

Block Assembly

1. Join 1 light print and 1 blue print A triangle to make 1 corner unit. Make 4 corner units.

2. Join 1 light print and 1 red print C rectangle to make 1 side unit. Make 4 side units.

3. Lay out corner units, side units and light print B square as shown in Churn Dash *Block Assembly Diagram* on page 68. Join into rows; join rows to complete 1 large Churn Dash block as shown in photo.

4. Add side borders. Add top and bottom borders.

PROJECT BY **Shelby Sawyer Morris**.

Slice of Lemon

Nothing brightens a table like a pretty runner. Here, Shelby Sawyer Morris combined classic blue and yellow prints that work perfectly for spring and summer months.

PROJECT RATING: INTERMEDIATE
Size: 23" × 44"
Blocks: 3 (9") blocks

MATERIALS

3 fat eighths★ assorted yellow prints for block backgrounds

6 fat eighths★ assorted blue prints for blocks

1 fat quarter★★ blue print #1 for sashing

½ yard blue print #2 for sashing squares and outer border

½ yard yellow check for sashing, middle border, and binding

¼ yard dark blue print for inner border

1¼ yards backing fabric

1 (25" × 46") piece batting

★fat eighth = 9" × 22"

★★fat quarter = 18" × 20"

Cutting

Measurements include ¼" seam allowances. Border strips are exact length needed. You may want to make them longer to allow for piecing variations.

From each yellow print fat eighth, cut:

- 1 (3"-wide) strip. From strip, cut 2 (3") squares. Cut squares in half diagonally to make 4 half-square B triangles.

- 1 (2⅜"-wide) strip. From strip, cut 4 (2⅜") squares. Cut squares in half diagonally to make 8 half-square D triangles.

- 1 (2"-wide) strip. From strip, cut 4 (2" × 3½") E rectangles.

From each of 3 blue print fat eighths, cut:

- 1 (3½"-wide) strip. From strip, cut 1 (3½") A square and 4 (2") F squares.

- 1 (2⅜"-wide) strip. From strip, cut 4 (2⅜") squares. Cut squares in half diagonally to make 8 half-square D triangles.

From each of 3 blue print fat eighths, cut:

- 1 (3⅞"-wide) strip. From strip, cut 2 (3⅞") squares. Cut squares in half diagonally to make 4 half-square C triangles.

From blue print #1 fat quarter, cut:

- 2 (6½"-wide) strips for strip sets.

From blue print #2, cut:

- 4 (3½"-wide) strips. From strips, cut 2 (3½" × 38½") side outer borders and 2 (3½" × 23½") top and bottom outer borders.

- 1 (2"-wide) strip. Cut strip in half to make 2 strips for strip set.

From yellow check, cut:

- 4 (2¼"-wide) strips for binding.

- 2 (2"-wide) strips. Cut strips in half to make 4 strips for strip sets.

- 3 (1"-wide) strips. From strips, cut 2 (1" × 37½") side middle borders and 2 (1" × 17½") top and bottom middle borders.

From dark blue print, cut:

- 3 (2½"-wide) strips. From strips, cut 2 (2½" × 33½") side inner borders and 2 (2½" × 16½") top and bottom inner borders.

Block Assembly

1. Lay out 1 blue print A square, 4 matching yellow print B triangles, and 4 matching blue print C triangles as shown in *Block Center Diagrams*. Join to complete 1 Block Center.

2. Join 1 blue print D triangle and 1 yellow print D triangle as shown in *Triangle-Square Diagrams*. Make 8 matching triangle-squares.

3. Add 2 triangle-squares to 1 yellow print E rectangle as shown in *Side Unit Diagrams*. Make 4 matching Side Units.

4. Lay out Block Center, 4 Side Units, and 4 blue print F squares as shown in *Block Assembly Diagram*. Join into rows; join rows to complete 1 block *(Block Diagram)*. Make 3 blocks.

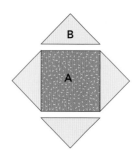

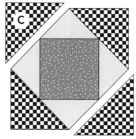

Block Center Diagrams

Triangle-Square Diagrams

Side Unit Diagrams

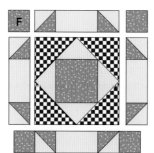

Block Assembly Diagram

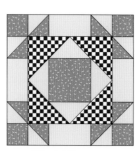

Block Diagram

Sashing Assembly

1. Join 1 blue print #1 strip and 2 yellow check strips as shown in *Strip Set #1 Diagram*. From strip set, cut 6 (2"-wide) #1 segments.

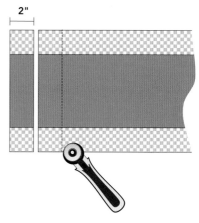

Strip Set #1 Diagram

2. Join 1 blue print #1 strip, 2 yellow check strips, and 3 blue print #2 strips as shown in *Strip Set #2 Diagram*. From strip set, cut 4 (2"-wide) #2 segments.

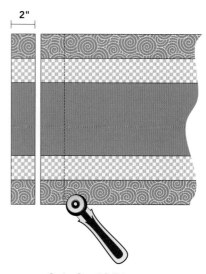

Strip Set #2 Diagram

Assembly Diagram

Quilt Assembly

1. Referring to *Assembly Diagram*, lay out blocks and strip set segments as shown. Join into rows; join rows to complete table runner center.

2. Add dark blue side inner borders to table runner center. Add dark blue top and bottom inner borders to table runner.

3. Repeat for yellow check middle borders and blue print outer borders.

Finishing

1. Layer backing, batting, and quilt top; baste. Quilt as desired. Quilt shown was quilted in the ditch in blocks, and with meandering in outer border.

2. Join 2¼"-wide yellow check strips into 1 continuous piece for straight-grain French-fold binding. Add binding to quilt.

TRIED & TRUE

This block was made in Morning Glory fabrics by Robyn Pandolph for Moda.

DESIGNER

Shelby Sawyer Morris is an accomplished quiltmaker from Cumming, Georgia. Her work has appeared several times in the pages of *Love of Quilting* magazine. ✳

Painted Desert

Designer Shon McMain says, "With accurate cutting and piecing, you can produce a miniature quilt that will be as visually striking and as dear to the heart as a large quilt." Try Shon's clever technique for making accurate star points.

PROJECT RATING: INTERMEDIATE
Size: 14¼" × 14¼"
Blocks: 13 (3") Ohio Star blocks

MATERIALS

13 (8") squares assorted medium and dark batiks
¾ yard tan batik
Paper for foundations
1 fat quarter★ backing fabric
18" square quilt batting
★fat quarter = 18" × 20"

Cutting

Paper piecing patterns for border are on page 77. Measurements include ¼" seam allowances.

From each medium/dark batik square, cut:
• 1 (2½") square. Cut square in half diagonally in both directions to make 4 quarter-square triangles for foundation piecing.
• 13 (1½") squares for blocks.

From tan batik, cut:
• 1 (5½"-wide) strip. From strip, cut 2 (5½") squares and 2 (3") squares. Cut 5½" squares in half diagonally in both directions to make 8 side setting triangles. Cut 3" squares in half diagonally to make 4 corner setting triangles.
• 2 (2¼"-wide) strips for binding.

- 7 (1½"-wide) strips. From strips, cut 104 (1½") squares and 56 (1½" × 2") rectangles for foundation piecing.

Block Assembly

1. Choose 1 set of 9 matching squares from 1 medium/dark batik, 4 matching squares of a contrasting batik, and 8 squares of tan batik.

2. Join 2 squares of 1 color, 1 square of contrasting color, and 1 tan square to make a Four Patch Unit as shown in *Star Point Unit Diagrams*.

3. To cut a 1½" star point unit, place the ¾" line of ruler over the center intersection of four patch with the 45-degree line of the ruler aligned with 1

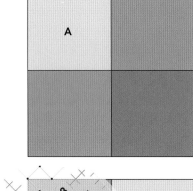

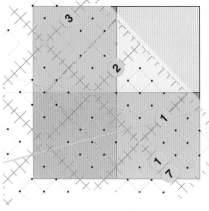

Star Point Unit Diagrams

side of the four patch. Trim off corner of four patch. Rotate unit and repeat on remaining corners to make 1 Star Point Unit. Make 4 Star Point Units.

4. Lay out 4 Star Point Units, 1 medium/dark square, and 4 tan squares as shown in *Block Assembly Diagram*. Join pieces into rows; join rows to complete 1 Ohio Star block *(Block Diagram)*. Make 13 blocks.

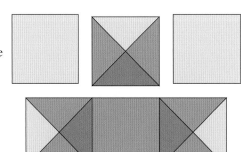

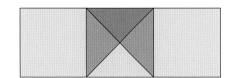

Block Assembly Diagram

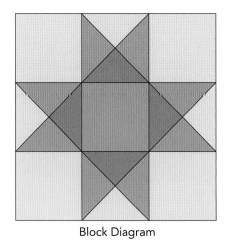

Block Diagram

Quilt Assembly

1. Lay out blocks, side setting triangles, and corner setting triangles as shown in *Quilt Top Assembly Diagram*. Join pieces into diagonal rows; join rows to complete quilt center.

2. Trace or photo copy 4 each of border sections A and B on page 77. Foundation piece sections in numerical order. Refer to *Quilt Top Assembly Diagram* for color placement.

3. Join 1 section A and 1 section B to make 1 border. Make 4 borders.

4. Measure side of quilt and trim 1 border strip to this length. Add border to side of quilt. Repeat for remaining side, top, and bottom of quilt.

Finishing

1. Layer backing, batting, and quilt top; baste. Quilt as desired. Quilt shown was quilted in the ditch in the blocks and with small stippling in the background.

2. Join 2¼"-wide tan strips into 1 continuous piece for straight-grain French-fold binding. Add binding to quilt.

DESIGNER

Whether she's choosing fabrics, creating original designs, piecing, or quilting, Shon McMain loves every aspect of making quilts. Her designs have appeared in many issues of *Love of Quilting*. She lives in West Des Moines, Iowa.

Section A   **Section B**

Quilt Top Assembly Diagram

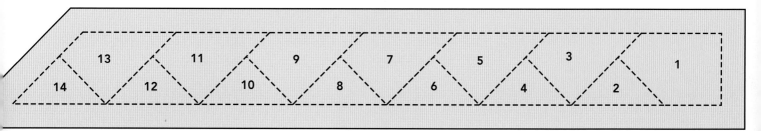

Border Section A

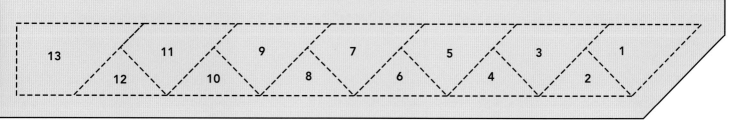

Border Section B

French Floral

Designer Patricia Elkovitch used print fabrics with a French color scheme to make this small quilt. It's great for use as a table topper or a wallhanging.

PROJECT RATING: INTERMEDIATE
Size: 39" × 39"
Blocks: 13 (5") 25 Patch blocks

MATERIALS

1⅝ yards beige print
5 fat eighths★ assorted light blue prints
5 fat eighths★ assorted dark blue prints
½ yard yellow print
1 fat eighth★ yellow solid
1 fat eighth★ red solid
¼ yard green print
¼ yard light blue print for piping
½ yard medium blue print for binding
Paper-backed fusible web
1¼ yards backing fabric
Crib-size quilt batting
★fat eighth = 9" × 20"

Cutting

Measurements include ¼" seam allowances. Border strips are exact length needed. You may want to make them longer to allow for piecing variations. Patterns for appliqué are on page 82. Follow manufacturer's instructions for using fusible web.

From beige print, cut:

- 2 (5½"-wide) strips. From strips, cut 12 (5½") F squares.
- 4 (3½"-wide) strips. From strips, cut 2 (3½" × 33½") side outer borders and 2 (3½" × 39½") top and bottom outer borders.
- 1 (2½"-wide) strip. Cut strip in half to make 2 (2½" × 20") strips for strip sets.
- 16 (1½"-wide) strips. From 7 strips, cut 8 (1½" × 10½") D rectangles, 4 (1½" × 9½") E rectangles, 12 (1½" × 5½") C rectangles, and 8 (1½" × 3½") B rectangles. Cut remaining strips in half to make 18 (1½" × 20") strips for strip sets.

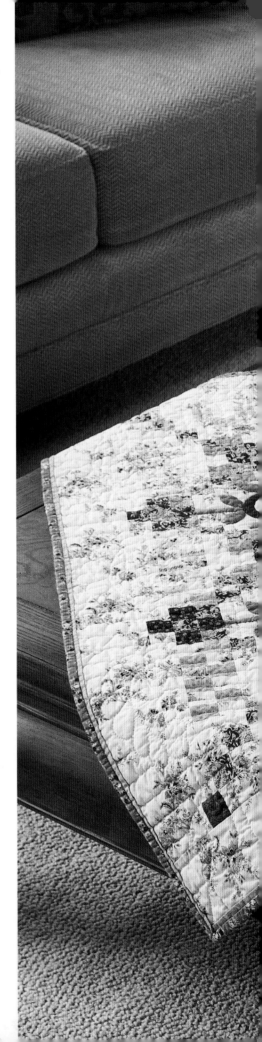

From each light blue print fat eighth, cut:

• 4 (1½"-wide) strips for strip sets.

From each dark blue print fat eighth, cut:

• 3 (1½"-wide) strips. From 1 strip, cut 3 (1½") A squares. Remaining strips are for strip sets.

From yellow print, cut:

• 10 (1½"-wide) strips. From 1 strip, cut 16 (1½") A squares. Cut remaining strips in half to make 18 (1½" × 20") strips for strip sets.

From yellow solid, cut:

• 12 Flower Centers.

From red solid, cut:

• 12 Flowers.

From green print, cut:

• 96 Leaves.

• 48 Stems.

From light blue print, cut:

• 4 (1"-wide) strips. From strips, cut 4 (1" × 39½") piping strips.

From medium blue print, cut:

• 5 (2¼"-wide) strips for binding.

Block Assembly

1. Join 2 (1½"-wide) yellow print strips, 2 (1½"-wide) matching light blue strips, and 1 (1½"-wide) beige print strip as shown in *Strip Set #1 Diagram*. Make 3 Strip Set #1. From strip sets, cut 13 sets of 2 matching (1½") #1 segments.

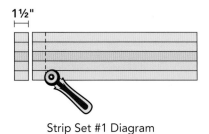

Strip Set #1 Diagram

2. Join 2 (1½"-wide) matching light blue print strips, 2 (1½"-wide) yellow print strips, and 1 (1½"-wide) dark blue print strip as shown in *Strip Set #2 Diagram*. Make 3 Strip Set #2. From strip sets, cut 13 sets of 2 matching (1½") #2 segments.

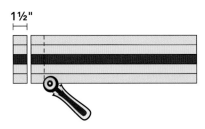

Strip Set #2 Diagram

3. Join 2 (1½"-wide) beige print strips, 2 (1½"-wide) matching dark blue print strips, and 1 (1½"-wide) yellow print strip as shown in *Strip Set #3 Diagram*. Make 2 Strip Set #3. From strip sets, cut 13 (1½") #3 segments.

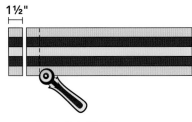

Strip Set #3 Diagram

4. Lay out 2 matching #1 segments, 2 matching #2 segments, and 1 #3 segment as shown in *Block Assembly Diagram*. Join segments to complete 1 block *(Block Diagram)*. Make 13 blocks.

Block Assembly Diagram

Block Diagram

Pieced Inner Border Assembly

1. Join 1 (1½"-wide) yellow print strip and 1 (2½"-wide) beige print strip as shown in *Strip Set #4 Diagram*. From strip set, cut 8 (1½") #4 segments.

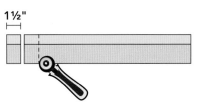

Strip Set #4 Diagram

2. Join 2 (1½"-wide) beige print strips and 1 (1½"-wide) yellow print strip as shown in *Strip Set #5 Diagram*. From strip set, cut 4 (1½") #5 segments.

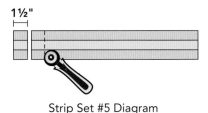

Strip Set #5 Diagram

3. Lay out 2 #4 segments and 1 #5 segment as shown in *Corner Unit Diagrams*. Join segments to complete 1 Corner Unit. Make 4 Corner Units.

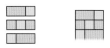

Corner Unit Diagrams

4. Join 1 (1½"-wide) light blue print strip and 1 (1½"-wide) beige print strip as shown in *Strip Set #6 Diagram*. Make 8 Strip Set #6. From strip sets, cut 12 sets of 5 matching (1½") #6 segments and 8 sets of 2 matching (1½") #6 segments.

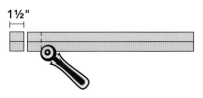

Strip Set #6 Diagram

5. Lay out 5 matching #6 segments and 1 beige print C rectangle as shown in *Border Unit #1 Diagrams*. Join to complete 1 Border Unit #1. Make 12 Border Unit #1.

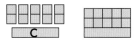

Border Unit #1 Diagrams

6. Join 1 (1½"-wide) dark blue print strip and 1 (1½"-wide) yellow print strip as shown in *Strip Set #7 Diagram*. Make 2 Strip Set #7. From strip sets, cut 12 sets of 2 matching (1½") #7 segments.

Strip Set #7 Diagram

7. Lay out 2 matching #6 segments, 3 matching #7 segments, 2 yellow print A squares, and 1 beige print B rectangle as shown in *Border Unit #2 Diagrams*. Join to complete 1 Border Unit #2. Make 8 Border Unit #2.

Border Unit #2 Diagrams

8. Lay out 3 Border Unit #1 and 2 Border Unit #2 as shown in *Quilt Top Assembly Diagram*. Join border units to make 1 pieced inner border. Make 4 pieced inner borders.

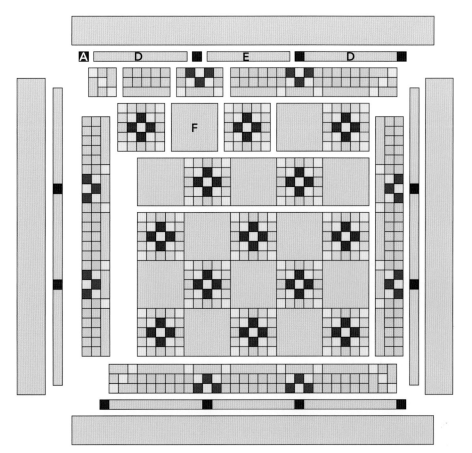

Quilt Top Assembly Diagram

Quilt Assembly

1. Lay out blocks and F squares as shown in *Quilt Top Assembly Diagram*. Join into rows; join rows to complete quilt center.

2. Add 1 pieced inner border to each side of quilt center.

3. Add 1 Corner Unit to each end of remaining pieced inner borders. Add borders to top and bottom of quilt.

4. Position Flowers, Flower Centers, Stems, and Leaves atop quilt center as shown in photo on page 83. Appliqué pieces on quilt top.

5. Lay out 2 beige print D rectangles, 1 beige print E rectangle, and 2 dark blue print A squares as shown in *Quilt Top Assembly Diagram*. Join to make 1 middle border. Make 4 middle borders.

6. Add 1 middle border to each side of quilt.

7. Add 1 dark blue print A square to each end of remaining middle borders. Add borders to top and bottom of quilt.

8. Add beige print side outer borders to quilt center. Add top and bottom outer borders to quilt.

> **Sew Smart**™
> Remove a few stitches in seams to tuck in ends of stems. Re-sew seams.
> —Marianne

Finishing

1. Layer backing, batting, and quilt top; baste. Quilt as desired. Quilt shown was outline quilted around appliqué, has straight lines in blocks and pieced borders, and has a feather design in the outer border *(Quilting Diagram)*.

2. Fold 1 light blue piping strip in half, wrong sides facing; press. Aligning raw edges, baste piping strip to 1 side of quilt. Repeat for opposite side and top and bottom of quilt.

3. Join 2¼"-wide medium blue print strips into 1 continuous piece for straight-grain French-fold binding. Add binding to quilt.

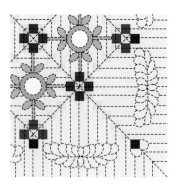

Quilting Diagram

DESIGNER

Patricia C. Elkovitch's family collects children's books, and she was reminded of *The Little Prince* when making this quilt with a French color scheme. Patricia, who lives in Skaneateles, New York, is passionate about women's history and nineteenth-century textiles. ✳

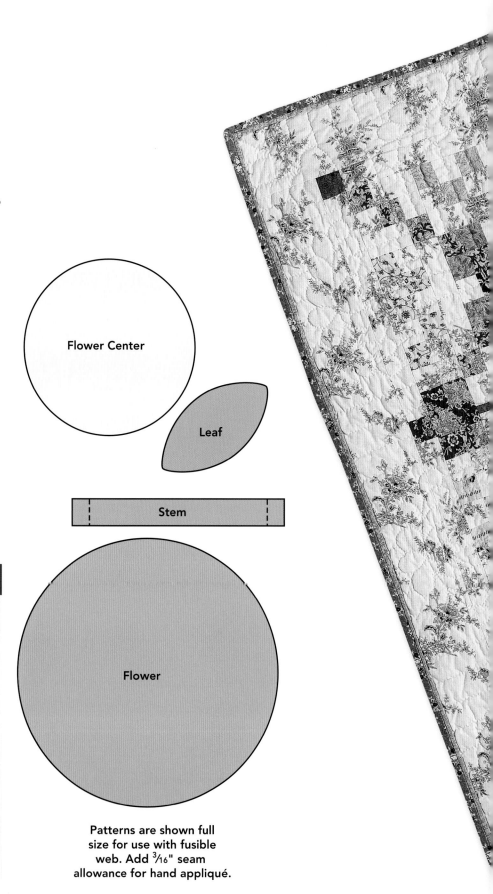

Flower Center

Leaf

Stem

Flower

Patterns are shown full size for use with fusible web. Add ³⁄₁₆" seam allowance for hand appliqué.

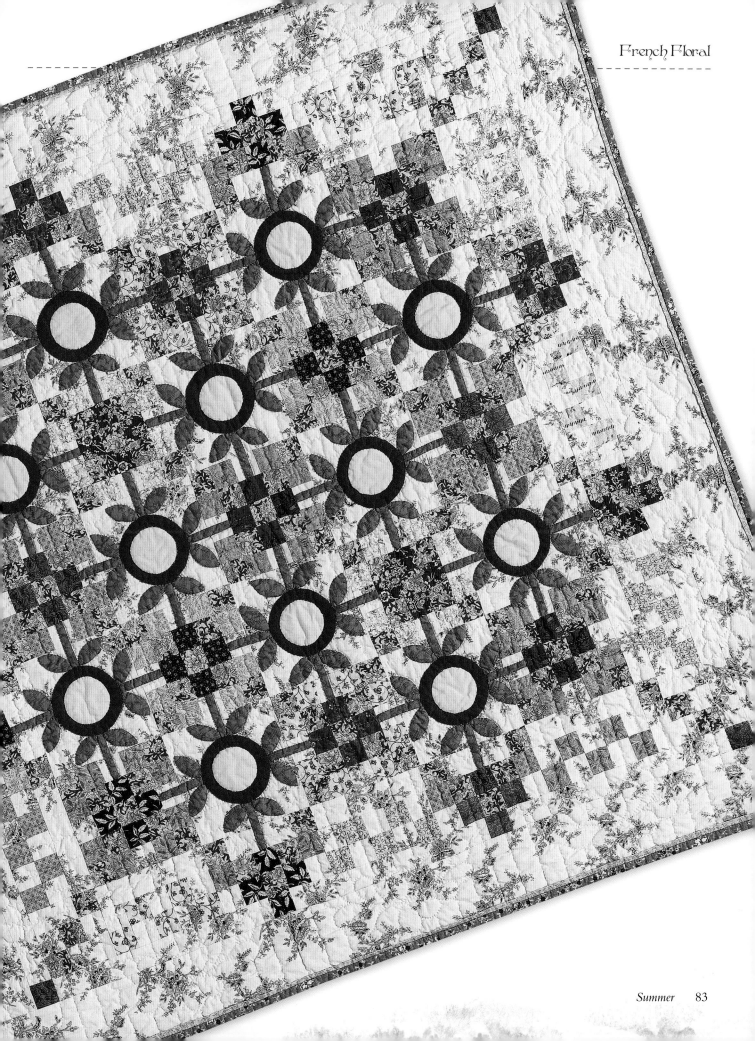

Prairie Wind

Perfect for everyday decorating, this cozy table runner combines piecing and appliqué in warm country colors.

PROJECT RATING: INTERMEDIATE
Size: 17" × 54"
Blocks: 1 (12") block

MATERIALS

¾ yard gold print
⅜ yard brown print
¼ yard medium blue print
¼ yard light blue print
1 fat eighth★ red print #1
1 fat eighth★ red print #2
½ yard green print
Paper-backed fusible web
1¼ yards backing fabric
Crib-size quilt batting
★fat eighth = 9" × 20"

Cutting

Measurements include ¼" seam allowances. Patterns for appliqué shapes are on page 88. Follow manufacturer's instructions for using fusible web.

From gold print, cut:

• 1 (12½"-wide) strip. From strip, cut 1 (12½") square. Cut square in half diagonally to make 2 half-square J triangles.
• 1 (9⅜"-wide) strip. From strip, cut 2 (9⅜") squares. Cut squares in half diagonally to make 4 half-square F triangles.
• 2 (4½"-wide) strips. From strips, cut 4 (4½" × 10½") I rectangles.
• 2 (3"-wide) strips. From strips, cut 16 (3") H squares.
• 1 (2½"-wide) strip. From strip, cut 4 (2½") A squares.
• 5 (1½"-wide) strips. From 3 strips, cut 8 (1½" × 4½") E rectangles, 8 (1½" × 3½") D rectangles, 8 (1½" × 2½") C rectangles, and 16 (1½") B squares. Remaining strips are for strip sets.

From brown print, cut:

- 1 (2½"-wide) strip. From strip, cut 4 (2½" × 3½") K rectangles.
- 4 (2¼"-wide) strips for binding.

From medium blue print, cut:

- 1 (2½"-wide) strip. From strip, cut 1 (2½") A square.
- 3 (1½"-wide) strips. From 1 strip, cut 20 (1½") B squares. Remaining strips are for strip sets.

From light blue print, cut:

- 1 (5½"-wide) strip. From strip, cut 4 (5½") G squares.

From red print #1, cut:

- 6 Flowers.

From red print #2, cut:

- 6 Flower Centers.

From green print, cut:

- 90" of (1⅛"-wide) bias strips for stems. Fold bias strips in thirds, press, and hand baste fold in place to prepare stems for appliqué.
- 16 Leaves.
- 6 Flower Leaves.

Center Unit Assembly

1. Lay out 5 medium blue print B squares, 2 gold print E rectangles, 2 gold print D rectangles, 2 gold print C rectangles, and 2 gold print D squares as shown in *Unit 1 Diagrams*. Join into rows; join rows to complete Unit 1. Make 4 Unit 1.

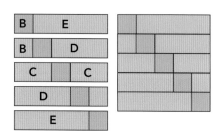

Unit 1 Diagrams

2. Referring to *Diagonal Seams Diagrams*, place 1 gold print B square atop 1 brown print K rectangle, right sides facing. Stitch diagonally from corner to corner as shown. Trim ¼" beyond stitching. Press open to reveal triangle. Repeat for adjacent corner to complete 1 Diagonal Seams Unit. Make 4 Diagonal Seams Units.

Diagonal Seams Diagrams

3. Join 1 Diagonal Seams Unit and 1 gold print A square as shown in *Unit 2 Diagrams*. Make 4 Unit 2.

Unit 2 Diagrams

4. Lay out 4 Unit 1, 4 Unit 2, and 1 medium blue print A square as shown in *Block Assembly Diagram*. Join pieces into rows; join rows to complete block *(Block Diagram)*.

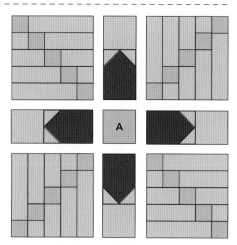

Block Assembly Diagram

Block Diagram

5. Referring to *Center Unit Assembly Diagram*, lay out block and 4 gold print F triangles as shown. Join to complete Center Unit.

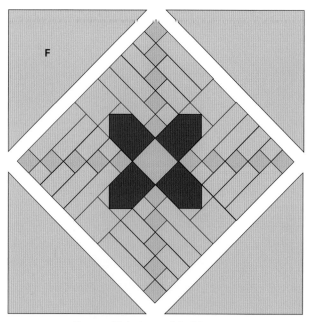

Center Unit Assembly Diagram

End Unit Assembly

1. Join 1 medium blue print strip and 1 gold print strip as shown in *Strip Set Diagram*. Make 2 strip sets. From strip sets, cut 40 (1½") segments.

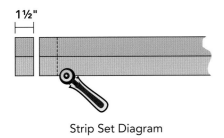

1½"

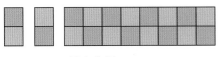

Strip Set Diagram

2. Join 10 strip set segments as shown in *Unit 3 Diagram*. Make 4 Unit 3.

Unit 3 Diagram

3. Referring to *Unit 4 Diagrams*, place 1 gold print H square atop 1 light blue print G square, right sides facing. Stitch diagonally from corner to corner as shown. Trim ¼" beyond stitching. Press open to reveal triangle. Repeat for 3 remaining corners to complete Unit 4. Make 4 Unit 4.

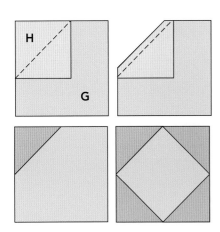

Unit 4 Diagrams

4. Lay out 2 Unit 4, 2 Unit 3, 2 gold print I rectangles, and 1 gold print J triangle as shown in *Assembly Diagram*. Join pieces to complete Table Runner End. Make 2 Table Runner Ends.

Table Runner Assembly

1. Join Center Unit and Table Runner Ends as shown in *Assembly Diagram*.

2. Referring to *Assembly Diagram*, arrange stems, leaves, and flower pieces atop table runner. Appliqué pieces in place.

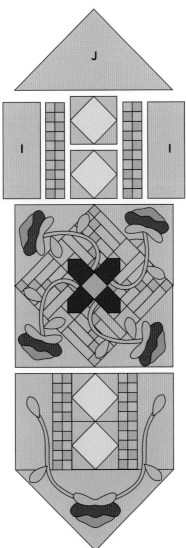

Assembly Diagram

Finishing

1. Divide backing into 2 (⅝-yard) lengths. Join panels along short edges.

2. Layer backing, batting, and quilt top; baste. Quilt as desired. Table runner shown was outline quilted around appliqué, and has freehand quilting in the gold background *(Quilting Diagram)*.

3. Join 2¼"-wide brown print strips into 1 continuous piece for straight-grain French-fold binding. Add binding to quilt.

Quilting Diagram

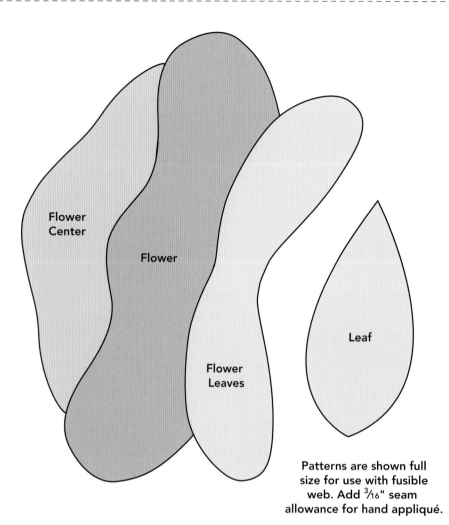

Flower Center

Flower

Flower Leaves

Leaf

Patterns are shown full size for use with fusible web. Add $^3/_{16}$" seam allowance for hand appliqué.

TRIED & TRUE

Create a primitive folk art look by using a dark background and strong colors. Fabrics shown are from the Fantasia collection by Red Rooster

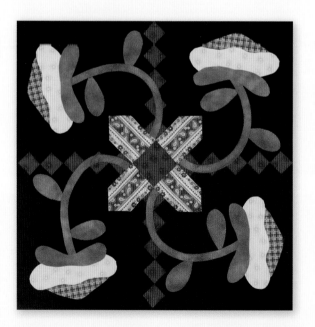

DESIGNER

Deanne Eisenman, a quilter and designer for over seventeen years, named her pattern company for her cat, Snuggles. Deanne lives in Osage, Iowa, with her husband and children. Her first book, *Country-Fresh Quilts*, was published by Martingale & Company in 2008. ✳

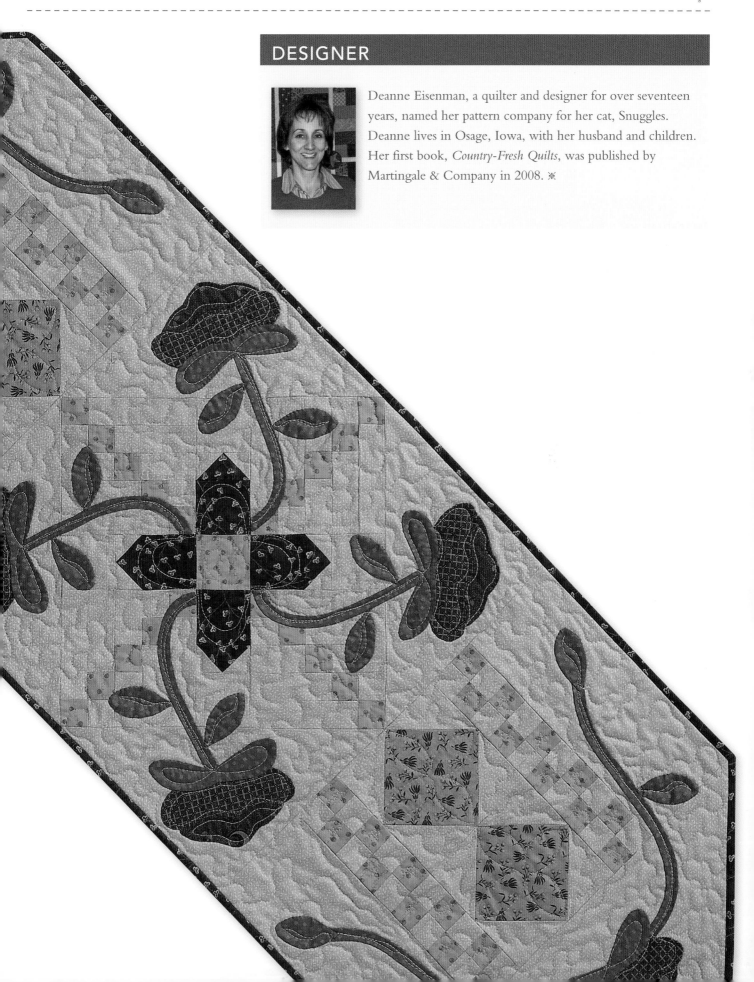

Fall

PROJECT BY **Carri Thompson and Kari Carr**.
MACHINE QUILTED BY **Rosalie Davenport**.

Fall's Finery

Designers Carri Thompson and Kari Carr combined piecing, wool appliqué, bead embellishments, and 3-D sunflowers in their seasonal quilt. Our *Sew Easy* lesson on page 97 teaches you a clever technique for making a perfectly mitered, scalloped border.

PROJECT RATING: INTERMEDIATE
Size: 38" × 38"
Blocks: 4 (12") Basket blocks

MATERIALS

¾ yard cream print
1½ yards brown print
2¾ yards green print
1 fat eighth★ orange felted wool
1 fat eighth★ dark orange felted wool
1 fat quarter★★ gold felted wool
3 (8") squares felted wool in green, brown, and dark brown
16 (⅜") oval orange beads
Orange, green, brown, and gold perle cotton
2½ yards backing fabric
Crib-size quilt batting
★fat eighth = 9" × 20"
★★fat quarter = 18" × 20"

Cutting

Measurements include ¼" seam allowances. Border strips are exact length needed. Make freezer paper templates from patterns on page 96. Press templates onto wool and cut out shapes from desired fabrics; remove paper.

From cream print, cut:
• 1 (9⅜"-wide) strip. From strip, cut 2 (9⅜") squares. Cut squares in half diagonally to make 4 half-square A triangles.
• 6 (2¼"-wide) strips. From 1 strip, cut 4 (2¼" × 4") C rectangles and 4 (2¼") D squares. Remaining strips are for binding.

From brown print, cut:
• 1 (12⅞"-wide) strip. From strip, cut 2 (12⅞") squares. Cut squares in half diagonally to make 4 half-square F triangles.
• 4 (6¾"-wide) strips. From strips, cut 2 (6¾" × 38¾") top and bottom borders and 2 (6¾" × 26¼") side borders.

- 2 (2¼"-wide) strips. From strips, cut 1 (2¼" × 26¼") horizontal sashing rectangle and 2 (2¼" × 12½") vertical sashing rectangles.

From green print, cut:

- 1 (4"-wide) strip. From strip, cut 4 (4") E squares.
- 2 (2¼"-wide) strips. From strips, cut 8 (2¼" × 9") B rectangles.

From remaining green print, cut:

- 4 (10"-wide) bias strips. From strips, cut 4 (10" × 38¾") border frame strips.

From orange wool, cut:

- 4 Pumpkin Centers.

From dark orange wool, cut:

- 4 Pumpkin Sides.
- 4 Pumpkin Sides reversed.

From green wool, cut:

- 4 Leaves.

From gold wool, cut:

- 10 Sunflowers.

From brown wool, cut:

- 4 Pumpkin Stems.

From dark brown wool, cut:

- 5 Sunflower Centers.

Block Assembly

1. Lay out 1 cream print A triangle, 2 green print B rectangles, 1 cream print C rectangle, and 1 cream print D square as shown in *Basket Block Assembly Diagrams*. Join into sections; join sections. Trim B rectangles as shown.

2. Place 1 green print E square atop basket unit, right sides facing. Stitch diagonally from corner to corner. Trim ¼" beyond stitching. Press open to reveal triangle.

3. Add 1 brown print F triangle to basket unit to complete 1 Basket block *(Basket Block Diagram)*. Make 4 Basket blocks.

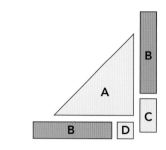

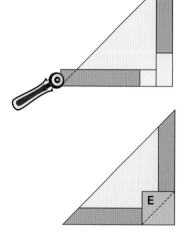

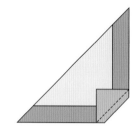

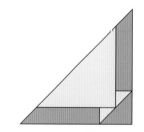

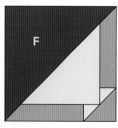

Basket Block Assembly Diagrams

Basket Block Diagram

Quilt Assembly

1. Lay out blocks and sashing rectangles as shown in *Quilt Top Assembly Diagram*. Join into rows; join rows to complete quilt center.

2. Add brown print side borders to quilt center. Add brown print top and bottom borders to quilt.

3. Referring to *Sew Easy: Scalloped Frame Border* on page 97, make frame using green print border frame strips.

Appliqué

1. Arrange pumpkin pieces and stems on quilt top as shown in photo on page 93. Blanket stitch in place using matching perle cotton *(Blanket Stitch Diagram)*.

2. Arrange leaves on pumpkins. Using backstitch and green perle cotton, stitch leaf veins, attaching leaves to quilt top *(Backstitch Diagrams)*.

3. Using green perle cotton, stem stitch vines *(Stem Stitch Diagram)*. Refer to photo on page 93 for placement.

4. Arrange lower sunflowers on quilt top; attach using gold perle cotton, stitching through center of each petal.

5. Arrange upper sunflowers and sunflower centers on quilt top. Using brown perle cotton, blanket stitch through all layers around sunflower center to attach sunflower center and upper petals.

Finishing

1. Divide backing into 2 (1¼-yard) lengths. Cut 1 piece in half lengthwise to make 2 narrow panels. Join 1 narrow panel to wider panel. Remaining panel is extra and can be used to make a hanging sleeve.

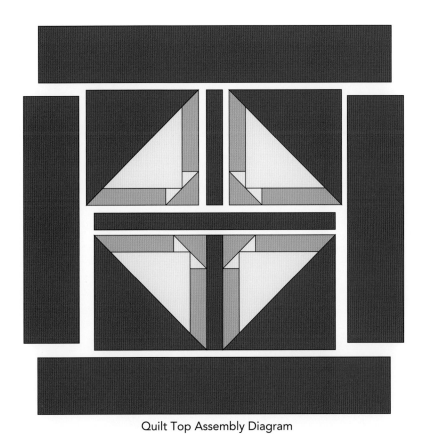

Quilt Top Assembly Diagram

2. Layer backing, batting, and quilt top; baste. Quilt as desired. Quilt shown was quilted with allover designs in the blocks and frame, leaving scallop unquilted *(Quilting Diagram)*.

3. Join 2¼"-wide cream print strips into 1 continuous piece for straight-grain French-fold binding. Add binding to quilt.

4. Add beads to quilt. Refer to photo on page 93 for placement.

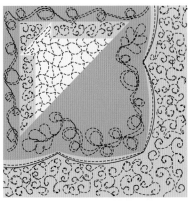

Quilting Diagram

STITCH DIAGRAMS

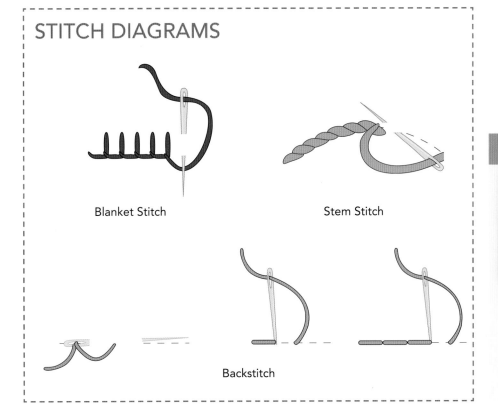

Blanket Stitch

Stem Stitch

Backstitch

DESIGNER

Carri Thompson and Kari Carr from Fergus Falls, Minnesota, call themselves "two recycled Home-Ec teachers." Together, they've created several patterns for New Leaf Stitches using their "Ah Ha—Perfect Mitered Corner" technique. ❋

Patterns are shown full size for use with fusible web. Add 3/16" seam allowance for hand appliqué.

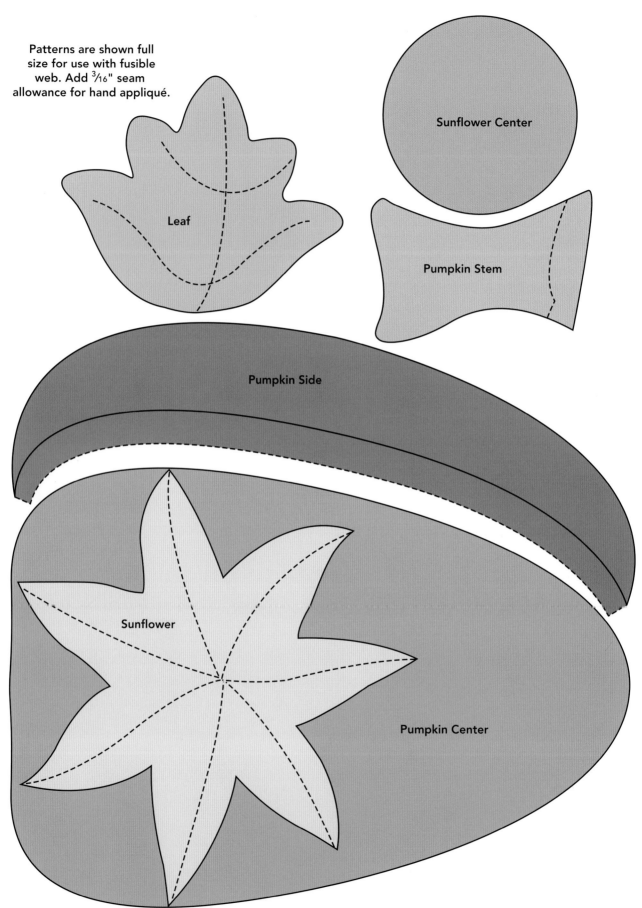

Leaf

Sunflower Center

Pumpkin Stem

Pumpkin Side

Sunflower

Pumpkin Center

Scalloped Frame Border

Use this technique to make a mitered border with a shallow "scallop" to frame any quilt.

A

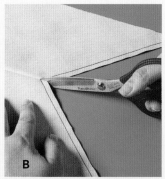

B

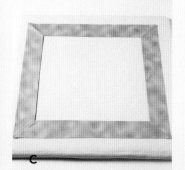

C

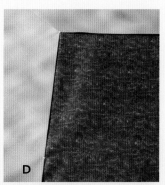

D

1. Fold bias borders in half lengthwise, wrong sides facing; press. Open fold.

> ## Sew Smart™
> When working with bias edges, handle carefully. —Marianne

2. On wrong side of 2 borders, mark a 45° angle from each corner to fold line (*Photo A*).

3. Place 1 marked border atop 1 unmarked border, right sides facing. At **one end**, stitch on marked line. Repeat for remaining border pair.

> ## Sew Smart™
> Decrease stitch length near the corner. —Marianne

4. In the same manner, join border pairs.

5. Trim ¼" beyond stitching; clip to point (*Photo B*).

> ## Sew Smart™
> Press side seams of "V" in opposite directions to reduce bulk. —Liz

6. Re-fold borders to complete border frame (*Photo C*).

7. Place frame atop quilt top, aligning raw edges. Baste through all layers close to outer edges.

8. Securely tack inside corners of frame and at points equal distance from corners (*Photo D*). For *Fall's Finery*, the distance is 9¼".

9. Turn back folded bias edges between tacks to create scallop; press (*Photo E*).

10. Stitch close to turned edge with straight or decorative stitch to hold in place (*Photo F*).

> ## Sew Smart™
> If desired, trim extra fabric from behind frame. —Liz

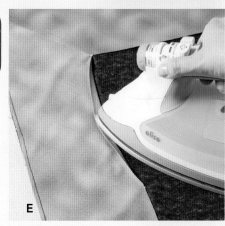

E

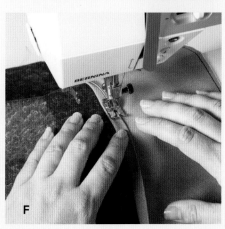

F

Chained Stars

Mother and daughter business partners Heather and Elissa Willms
each chose different fabrics to reflect her personal style. Make your table runner
using the Fons & Porter Flying Geese Ruler to easily cut triangles for Flying Geese.
Refer to *Sew Easy: Making Flying Geese Units* on page 47.

Size: 24" × 56"
Blocks: 3 (8") Star blocks

MATERIALS

1 yard brown print
⅝ yard green print
¾ yard turquoise print
½ yard cream print
Fons & Porter Flying Geese Ruler
   (optional)
1⅝ yards backing fabric
Crib-size quilt batting

Cutting

Measurements include ¼" seam
allowances. Border strips are exact
length needed. You may want to make
them longer to allow for piecing
variations.

Sew Smart™

To cut both kinds of triangles (E and F)
from the same size strips for the Flying
Geese Units, using the Fons & Porter
Flying Geese Ruler, see *Sew Easy:
Making Flying Geese Units* on page
47. If you are not using the Fons &
Porter Flying Geese Ruler, use the
cutting NOTE instructions given here.
—Marianne

From brown print, cut:

- 1 (4½"-wide) strip. From strip, cut 6
  (4½") A squares.
- 5 (3½"-wide) strips. From strips, cut
  2 (3½" × 24½") top and bottom
  outer borders. Piece remaining strips
  to make 2 (3½" × 50½") side outer
  borders.
- 2 (2½"-wide) strips. From strips, cut
  24 (2½") B squares.
- 1 (1½"-wide) strip. From strip, cut 4
  (1½" × 2½") C rectangles and 4 (1½"
  × 4½") D rectangles.
- 1 (2½"-wide) strip. From strip, cut 8 F
  "sky" triangles.
  NOTE: If not using the Fons & Porter
  Flying Geese Ruler, cut: 1 (2⅞"-wide)
  strip. From strip, cut 4 (2⅞") squares.

Cut squares in half diagonally to make
8 half-square F triangles.

From green print, cut:

- 1 (2½"-wide) strip. From strip, cut
  3 (2½") B squares.
- 8 (1½"-wide) strips. From strips, cut
  2 (1½" × 18½") top and bottom
  inner borders. Piece remaining strips
  to make 2 (1½" × 48½") side inner
  borders. Remaining strips are for
  strip sets.

From turquoise print, cut:

- 1 (4½"-wide) strip. From strip, cut
  6 (4½") A squares.
- 2 (2½"-wide) strips. From strips, cut
  24 (2½") B squares.
- 4 (2¼"-wide) strips for binding.
- 1 (1½"-wide) strip. From strip, cut
  2 (1½" × 2½") C rectangles and
  2 (1½" × 4½") D rectangles.
- 1 (2½"-wide) strip. From strip, cut
  16 F "sky" triangles.
  NOTE: If not using the Fons & Porter
  Flying Geese Ruler, cut: 1 (2⅞"-wide)
  strip. From strip, cut 8 (2⅞") squares.
  Cut squares in half diagonally to make
  16 half-square F triangles.

From cream print, cut:

- 1 (2½"-wide) strip. From strip, cut 12 (2½") B squares.
- 4 (1½"-wide) strips for strip sets.
- 2 (2½"-wide) strips. From strips, cut 12 E "goose" triangles.
  NOTE: If not using the Fons & Porter Flying Geese Ruler, cut: 1 (5¼"-wide) strip. From strip, cut 3 (5¼") squares. Cut squares in half diagonally in both directions to make 12 quarter-square E triangles.

Block Assembly

1. Join brown print C rectangles to top and bottom of 1 green print B square as shown in *Block Center Diagrams*. Add brown print D rectangles to sides to complete 1 Block Center. Make 2 brown Block Centers.

Block Center Diagrams

2. In the same manner, make 1 turquoise Block Center using turquoise print C and D rectangles.

3. Referring to *Sew Easy: Making Flying Geese Units* on page 47, join 2 turquoise print F triangles and 1 cream print E triangle to make a Flying Geese Unit *(Flying Geese Unit Diagram)*. Make 8 turquoise Flying Geese Units.

Flying Geese Unit Diagram

4. In the same manner, make 4 brown Flying Geese Units using brown print F triangles.

5. Lay out 1 brown Block Center, 4 turquoise Flying Geese Units, and 4

cream print B squares as shown in *Block Assembly Diagram*. Join into rows; join rows to complete 1 Star block *(Block Diagram)*. Make 2 turquoise Star blocks.

Block Assembly   Block Diagram
Diagram

6. In the same manner, make 1 brown Star block using brown Flying Geese Units and turquoise Block Center.

Table Runner Assembly

1. Join 1 (1½"-wide) cream print strip and 1 (1½"-wide) green print strip as shown in *Strip Set Diagram*. Make 4 strip sets. From strip sets, cut 96 (1½"-wide) segments.

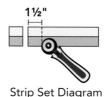

Strip Set Diagram

2. Referring to *Four Patch Diagrams*, join 2 segments to complete 1 Four Patch Unit. Make 48 Four Patch Units.

Four Patch Diagrams

3. Lay out 1 brown print A square, 1 turquoise print A square, 4 Four Patch Units, 2 brown print B squares, and 2 turquoise print B squares as shown in *Chain Row Diagrams*. Join to complete 1 Chain Row. Make 6 Chain Rows.

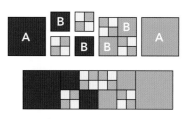

Chain Row Diagrams

4. Lay out 2 brown print B squares, 2 turquoise print B squares, and 4 Four Patch Units as shown in *Side Unit Diagrams*. Join to make 1 Side Unit. Make 6 Side Units.

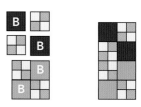

Side Unit Diagrams

Quilt Top Assembly Diagram

5. Lay out Chain Rows, Star Blocks, and Side Units as shown in *Quilt Top Assembly Diagram*. Join into rows; join rows to complete table runner center.

6. Add green print side inner borders to table runner center. Add green print top and bottom inner borders.

7. Repeat for brown print outer borders.

Finishing

1. Layer backing, batting, and quilt top; baste. Quilt as desired. Quilt shown was quilted in the ditch and with diagonal lines in the outer border *(Quilting Diagram)*.

2. Join 2¼"-wide turquoise print strips into 1 continuous piece for straight-grain French-fold binding. Add binding to quilt.

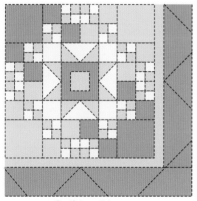

Quilting Diagram

DESIGNER

At age 15, Elissa Willms was inspired by the Elm Creek Quilt series to open Hopscotch Quilt Shop in Coaldale, Alberta. Her mother and business partner, Heather Willms, does the ordering and kitting, and writes all of the shop's patterns. Look for their book *Christmas Quilts From Hopscotch* at your local quilt shop. ✳

Falling Leaves

A checkerboard center of neutral prints makes the perfect backdrop for classic fall leaf colors. Machine appliqué the leaves with a satin or blanket stitch; or, for perfect blanket stitching with an embroidery machine, download our digitized design file at fonsandporter.com/fallingleaves.

PROJECT RATING: INTERMEDIATE
Size: 17" × 41"

MATERIALS

⅜ yard beige print #1

⅜ yard beige print #2

⅞ yard leaf print for border and binding

12" square green print for leaves

6" square red print for leaves

8" square rust print for leaves

8" square gold print for leaf and acorns

6" square light brown print for leaf and acorns

Paper-backed fusible web

1¼ yards backing fabric

21" × 45" rectangle quilt batting

Cutting

Measurements include ¼" seam allowances. Patterns for leaves and acorns are on pages 104 and 105. Follow manufacturer's instructions for using fusible web. Refer to *Sew Easy: Windowing Fusible Appliqué* on page 157.

From each beige print, cut:
• 3 (3½"-wide) strips for strip sets.

From leaf print border fabric, cut:
• 3 (4½"-wide) strips. From strips, cut 2 (4½" × 33½") top and bottom borders and 2 (4½" × 17½") side borders.
• 4 (2¼"-wide) strips for binding.

From green print, cut:
• 1 Leaf 1.
• 1 Leaf 2.
• 1 Leaf 3.

From red print, cut:
• 1 Leaf 2.
• 1 Leaf 5.

From rust print, cut:
• 1 Leaf 1.
• 2 Leaf 2 reversed.

From gold print, cut:
• 1 Leaf 4.
• 3 Caps.

From light brown print, cut:
• 1 Leaf 1.
• 3 Acorns.

Background Assembly

1. Join 3½"-wide beige print strips as shown in *Strip Set Diagrams* to make 1 Strip Set A and 1 Strip Set B.

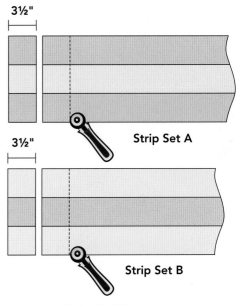

Strip Set A

Strip Set B

Strip Set Diagrams

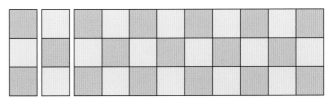

Quilt Center Assembly Diagram

2. From Strip Set A, cut 6 (3½"-wide) segments. From Strip Set B, cut 5 (3½"-wide) segments.

3. Lay out segments as shown in *Quilt Center Assembly Diagram*; join segments to complete center.

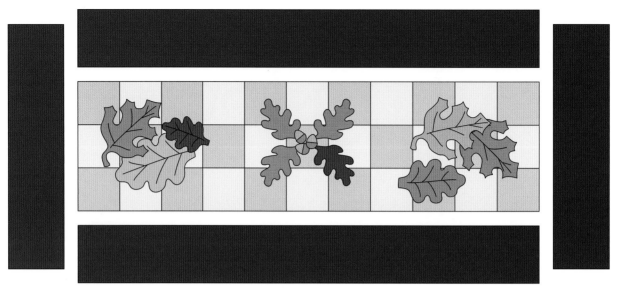

Quilt Assembly Diagram

Quilt Assembly

1. Arrange leaves and acorns on background. Fuse in place. Using black thread, machine blanket stitch around appliqués. Satin stitch veins. For hand appliqué, use blanket stitch around appliqués and outline stitch for veins (*Stitch Diagrams*).

Blanket Stitch Diagram

Outline Stitch Diagram

2. Add top and bottom borders to quilt. Add side borders to quilt.

Sew **Smart**™

For embroidery machine appliqué, position background fabric in hoop. Stitch thread color 1 to create a straight stitch outline to aid in positioning appliqué pieces. Without removing the project from the embroidery hoop, position and fuse leaves within stitching outlines. Stitch thread color 2 to appliqué around pieces and add veins to leaves. —Faith

Finishing

1. Layer backing, batting, and quilt top; baste. Quilt as desired. Quilt shown was quilted in the ditch in the center section and outline quilted around appliqués.

2. Join 2¼"-wide leaf print strips into 1 continuous piece for straight-grain French-fold binding. Add binding to quilt.

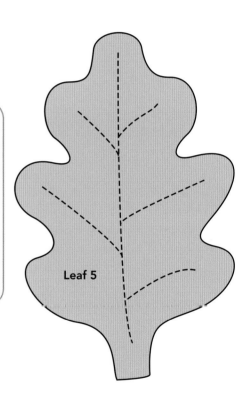

Leaf 5

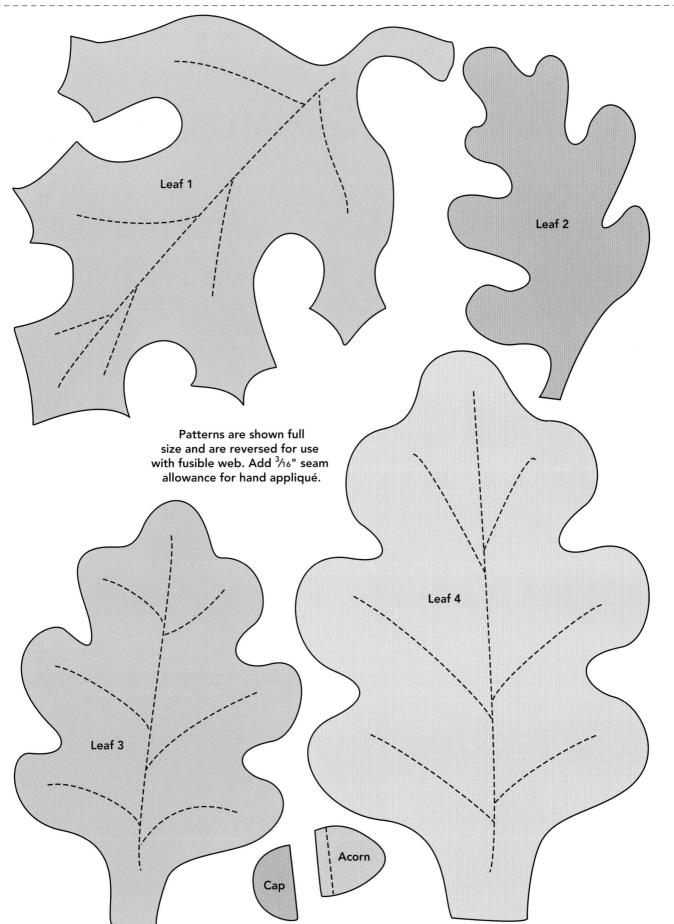

Leaf 1

Leaf 2

Patterns are shown full
size and are reversed for use
with fusible web. Add $\frac{3}{16}$" seam
allowance for hand appliqué.

Leaf 4

Leaf 3

Cap

Acorn

Infinity Blocks

The blocks in designer Lonni Rossi's contemporary quilt appear plugged into each other, creating a textured, woven look. Strip set construction makes this quilt go together quickly.

PROJECT RATING: EASY
Size: 52" × 52"
Blocks: 36 (7") Patch blocks

MATERIALS

½ yard black print #1 for strip sets
½ yard black print #2 for strip sets
¼ yard light brown print #1 for strip sets
¼ yard light brown print #2 for blocks
⅝ yard tan print for blocks
⅛ yard gold print #1 for strip sets
⅝ yard gold print #2 for blocks
½ yard rust print #1 for blocks
1⅜ yards rust print #2 for outer border and binding
3¼ yards backing fabric
Twin-size quilt batting

Cutting

Measurements include ¼" seam allowances. Border strips are exact length needed. You may want to make them longer to allow for piecing variations.

From black print #1, cut:

• 2 (3½"-wide) strips for strip sets.

• 4 (1½"-wide) strips for strip sets.

From black print #2, cut:

• 1 (3½"-wide) strip for strip sets.

• 2 (1½"-wide) strips for strip sets.

• 5 (1"-wide) strips. Piece strips to make 4 (1" × 42½") accent strips.

From light brown print #1, cut:

• 4 (1½"-wide) strips for strip sets.

From light brown print #2, cut:

• 4 (1½"-wide) strips for strip sets.

From tan print, cut:

• 1 (3½"-wide) strip for strip sets.

• 4 (2¼"-wide) strips for strip sets.

• 2 (1½"-wide) strips for strip sets.

From gold print #1, cut:

• 2 (1½"-wide) strips for strip sets.

From gold print #2, cut:

• 1 (3½"-wide) strip for strip sets.

• 4 (2¼"-wide) strips for strip sets.

• 2 (1½"-wide) strips for strip sets.

From rust print #1, cut:

• 1 (7½"-wide) strip. From strip, cut 4 (7½") G squares.

• 4 (1½"-wide) strips for strip sets.

From rust print #2, cut:

• 5 (5½"-wide) strips. Piece strips to make 2 (5½" × 42½") side borders and 2 (5½" × 52½") top and bottom borders.

• 6 (2¼"-wide) strips for binding.

Strip Set Assembly

1. Join 2 (1½"-wide) black print #1 strips, 2 (1½"-wide) light brown print #1 strips, and 1 (3½"-wide) black print #1 strip as shown in *Strip Set A Diagram*. Make 2 Strip Set A. From strip sets, cut 8 (7½"-wide) A segments.

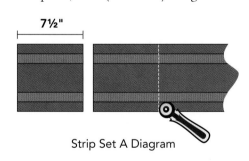

Strip Set A Diagram

2. Join 2 (1½"-wide) tan print strips, 2 (1½"-wide) light brown print #2 strips, and 1 (3½"-wide) tan print strip as shown in *Strip Set B Diagram*. From strip set, cut 18 (1¾"-wide) B segments.

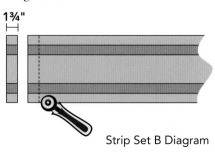

Strip Set B Diagram

3. Join 2 (1½"-wide) black print #2 strips, 2 (1½"-wide) gold print #1 strips, and 1 (3½"-wide) black print #2 strip as shown in *Strip Set C Diagram*. From strip set, cut 5 (7½"-wide) C segments.

7½"

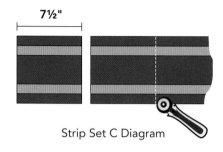

Strip Set C Diagram

4. Join 2 (1½"-wide) gold print #2 strips, 2 (1½"-wide) rust print #1 strips, and 1 (3½"-wide) gold print #2 strip as shown in *Strip Set D Diagram*. From strip set, cut 20 (1¾"-wide) D segments.

1¾"

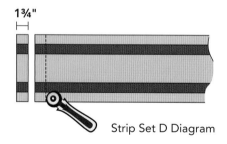

Strip Set D Diagram

5. Join 2 (2¼"-wide) gold print #2 strips and 1 (1¼"-wide) rust print #1 strip as shown in *Strip Set E Diagram*. Make 2 Strip Set E. From strip sets, cut 10 (7½"-wide) E segments.

7½"

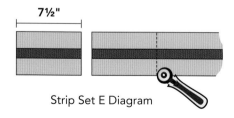

Strip Set E Diagram

6. Join 2 (2¼"-wide) tan print strips and 1 (1½"-wide) light brown print #2 strip as shown in *Strip Set F Diagram*. Make 2 Strip Set F. From strip sets, cut 9 (7½"-wide) F segments.

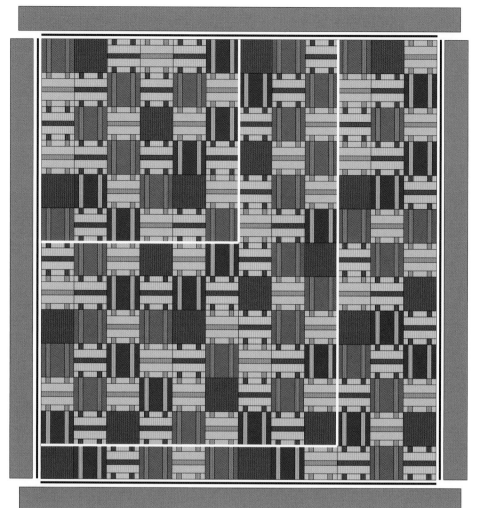

Quilt Top Assembly Diagram

7½"

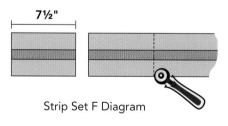

Strip Set F Diagram

Block Assembly

1. Lay out 2 D segments and 1 E segment as shown in *Gold Block Assembly Diagram*. Join pieces to complete 1 gold block *(Gold Block Diagram)*. Make 10 gold blocks.

2. Lay out 2 B segments and 1 F segment as shown in *Tan Block Assembly Diagram*. Join pieces to complete 1 tan block *(Tan Block Diagram)*. Make 9 tan blocks.

Gold Block
Assembly Diagram

Gold Block
Diagram

Tan Block
Assembly Diagram

Tan Block
Diagram

Quilt Assembly

1. Lay out blocks, A segments, C segments, and G squares as shown in *Quilt Top Assembly Diagram*. Join into

CHART FOR ALTERNATE SIZES

Size	Throw (73″ × 94″)	Queen (94″ × 101″)
Blocks	108	156
Setting	9 × 12	12 × 13
Materials	1 yard black print #1	1½ yards black print #1
	1 yard black print #2	1⅜ yards black print #2
	½ yard light brown print #1	¾ yard light brown print #1
	½ yard light brown print #2	⅝ yard light brown print #2
	1⅜ yards tan print	1⅝ yards tan print
	⅜ yard gold print #1	½ yard gold print #1
	1⅜ yards gold print #2	1⅝ yards gold print #2
	1¼ yards rust print #1	1¾ yards rust print #1
	2⅛ yards rust print #2	2½ yards rust print #2
	5¾ yards backing fabric	8⅝ yards backing fabric
	Full-size batting	King-size batting
Blocks/Strip Set Segments		
Gold Blocks	28	40
Tan Blocks	27	38
A Segments	24	34
C Segments	15	23
Rust G Squares	14	21

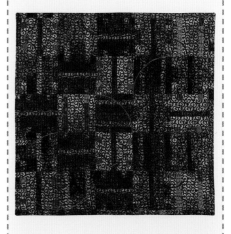
DESIGNER

A graphic designer who became an award-winning quilt artist, Lonni Rossi combines a love of communication through typography and the written word with a passion for textiles and surface design. ✳

horizontal rows; join rows to complete quilt center.

2. Press black print #2 accent strips in half lengthwise. Align raw edges of 1 folded strip with 1 side of quilt center; pin or baste in place. Repeat for remaining sides.

3. Add side borders to quilt center. Add top and bottom borders to quilt.

Finishing

1. Divide backing fabric into 2 (1⅝-yard) pieces. Cut 1 piece in half lengthwise. Sew 1 narrow panel to 1 side of wider panel. Press seam allowances toward narrow panel. Remaining panel is extra and can be used to make a hanging sleeve.

2. Layer backing, batting, and quilt top; baste. Quilt as desired. Quilt shown was quilted in the ditch.

3. Join 2¼"-wide rust print #2 strips into 1 continuous piece for straight-grain French-fold binding. Add binding to quilt.

PROJECT BY **Pat Sloan**.

Candy Corn

Designer Pat Sloan says she knows fall has arrived when she starts to see candy corn in stores. Her wool penny rug with candy corn motifs is quick and easy to make. Stitch it up in no time at all to decorate for Halloween.

PROJECT RATING: EASY

Size: 14" × 22"

MATERIALS

11" × 42" rectangle black felted wool for background and tongues

6" × 20" rectangle orange felted wool for stars, pennies, and candy corn bottoms

5" × 7" rectangle yellow felted wool for candy corn middles

4" × 5" rectangle white felted wool for candy corn tips

11" × 22" rectangle black cotton for lining

Size 8 perle cotton or embroidery floss in black, orange, gold, and cream

Cutting

Make freezer paper templates from patterns on page 113. Press templates onto wool and cut out shapes from desired fabrics; remove paper.

From black wool, cut:

• 1 Background oval.

• 16 Tongues.

From orange wool, cut:

• 16 Pennies.

• 5 Stars.

• 5 Candy Corn Bottoms.

From yellow wool, cut:

• 5 Candy Corn Middles.

From white wool, cut:

• 5 Candy Corn Tips.

From black cotton, cut:

• 1 lining oval.

Candy Corn Table Topper Diagram

Assembly

1. Center 1 orange Penny on the end of each Tongue. Blanket stitch with black perle cotton as shown in *Blanket Stitch Diagram*

Blanket Stitch Diagram

2. Blanket stitch around curved sides of each tongue with black perle cotton. Do not stitch on the straight side.

3. Referring to *Candy Corn Table Topper Diagram*, position stars on background. Blanket stitch around stars with orange perle cotton.

4. Position Bottoms, Middles, and Tips of candy corn pieces on background. (You may want to overlap them about ⅛".) Blanket stitch with matching perle cotton.

5. Place lining atop the table topper, right sides facing, and stitch around outside edge, leaving an opening 3" long on one side for turning. Turn right side out; press.

6. Blanket stitch with black perle cotton around outside edge of table topper. This will also close the opening used for turning.

7. Position Tongues around outside edge of table topper with ¼" of Tongue extending under edge. Whipstitch Tongues to the lining.

DESIGNER

Pat Sloan is a nationally-known quilt designer and teacher who specializes in folk-art appliqué.

※

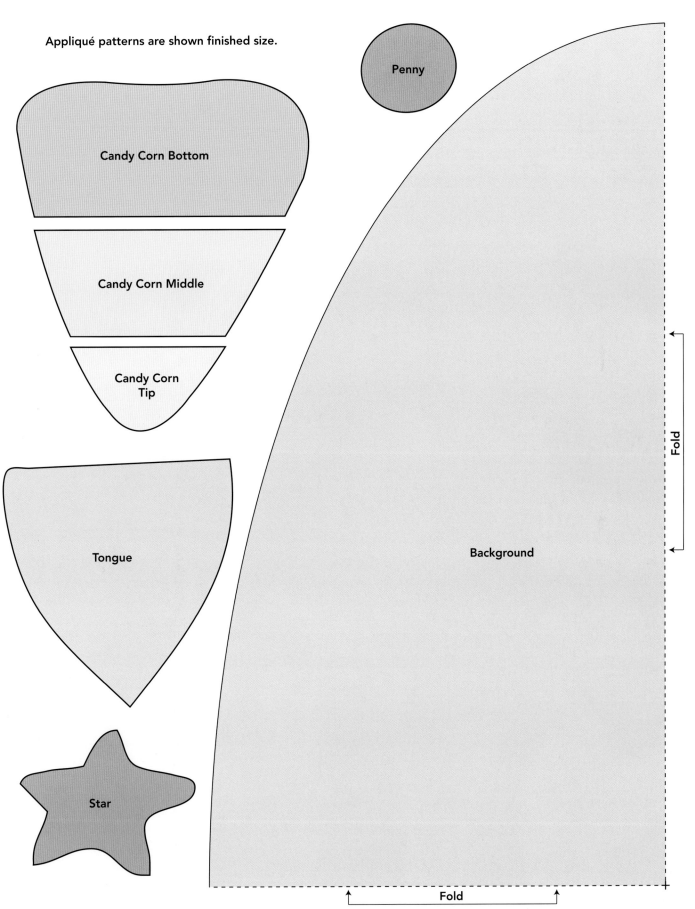

Appliqué patterns are shown finished size.

Penny

Candy Corn Bottom

Candy Corn Middle

Candy Corn Tip

Tongue

Background

Fold

Star

Fold

Prairie Cabin Mini

Jo Morton has made dozens of Log Cabin quilts, playing with different sets, numbers of blocks, and border treatments. Miniatures are favorites with Jo because she can hand quilt them in no time at all.

Size: 13½" × 18¼"

Blocks: 6 (4¾") Log Cabin blocks

MATERIALS

6" square red solid for block centers

6 (1" × 40") strips assorted light prints for blocks

6 (1" × 40") strips assorted dark prints for blocks

2 (1½" × 40") strips each of red print and brown print for border

¼ yard red-and-black check for binding

18" × 22" rectangle of backing fabric

18" × 22" rectangle of quilt batting

Cutting

Measurements include ¼" seam allowances.

From red solid, cut:

• 6 (1¼") center squares.

From each light print strip, cut:

• 1 (1" × 1¼") #1 rectangle.

• 1 (1" × 1¾") #2 rectangle.

• 1 (1" × 2¼") #5 rectangle.

• 1 (1" × 2¾") #6 rectangle.

• 1 (1" × 3¼") #9 rectangle.

• 1 (1" × 3¾") #10 rectangle.

• 1 (1" × 4¼") #13 rectangle.

• 1 (1" × 4¾") #14 rectangle.

From each dark print strip, cut:

• 1 (1" × 1¾") #3 rectangle.

• 1 (1" × 2¼") #4 rectangle.

• 1 (1" × 2¾") #7 rectangle.

• 1 (1" × 3¼") #8 rectangle.

• 1 (1" × 3¾") #11 rectangle.

• 1 (1" × 4¼") #12 rectangle.

• 1 (1" × 4¾") #15 rectangle.

• 1 (1" × 5¼") #16 rectangle.

From red-and-black check, cut:

• 80" of (2¼"-wide) bias strips. Join strips to make bias binding.

Block Assembly

1. Lay out pieces as shown in *Block Diagram*.

2. Join strips in numerical order to complete 1 Log Cabin block. Make 6 blocks.

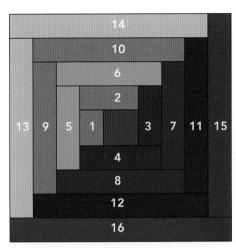

Block Diagram

Quilt Assembly

1. Lay out blocks as shown in *Quilt Top Assembly Diagram*.

2. Join blocks into rows; join rows to complete quilt center.

Quilt Top Assembly Diagram

3. Join 1 red print and 1 brown print strip as shown in *Strip Set Diagram*. Make 2 strip sets.

Strip Set Diagram

4. From strip sets, cut 2 (14¾"-long) side borders and 2 (14"-long) top and bottom borders.

5. Add side borders to quilt center. Add top and bottom borders to quilt.

Finishing

1. Layer backing, batting, and quilt top; baste. Quilt as desired. Quilt shown was hand quilted with concentric squares in the blocks and a diagonal grid in the border.

2. Add binding to quilt.

DESIGNER

Jo Morton began making quilts in 1980, and hasn't put down her needle since. A quilt artist, author, teacher, and lecturer, Jo designs fabrics for Andover Fabrics. She loves to make quilts in the spirit of the nineteenth century. Jo lives in Nebraska City, Nebraska, with her husband, Russ. ✳

Pineapple
Table Runner

A symbol of hospitality, the pineapple motif appears in many home decorating items. Julie Larsen used her method for making Pineapple blocks to create this table runner.

PROJECT RATING: INTERMEDIATE

Size: 17" × 51"

Blocks: 3 (12") Pineapple blocks
1 (12½") Setting block

MATERIALS

4 fat eighths★ assorted red prints for block corners

4 fat quarters★★ assorted tan prints for block backgrounds

¾ yard red print #1 for block centers, outside corners, and binding

1½ yards backing fabric

21" x 55" rectangle of quilt batting

★fat eighth = 9" × 20"

★★fat quarter = 18" × 20"

Cutting

Measurements include ¼" seam allowances. Because there are so many pieces which are similar in size, you may want to label them as you cut.

From each red print fat eighth, cut the following for block corners:

- 4 (3½") E squares.
- 4 (3") D squares.
- 4 (2½") C squares.
- 4 (1½") B squares.

From each tan print fat quarter, cut:

- 9 (1½"-wide) strips. From strips, cut:
  - 2 (1½" × 12½") K rectangles.
  - 3 (1½" × 10½") J rectangles.
  - 3 (1½" × 8½") I rectangles.
  - 3 (1¼" × 6¼") H rectangles.
  - 2 (1½" × 4½") G rectangles.
  - 1 (1½" × 13") Q rectangle.
  - 1 (1½" × 11") P rectangle.
  - 1 (1½" × 9") O rectangle.
  - 1 (1½" × 7") N rectangle.
  - 1 (1½" × 5") M rectangle.

(You will have a few extra pieces.)

From red print #1, cut:

- 1 (5"-wide) strip. From strip, cut 1 (5") L square and 3 (4½") A squares.
- 2 (4"-wide) strips. From strips, cut 16 (4") F squares.
- 5 (2¼"-wide) strips for binding.

Block Assembly

1. Referring to *Center Unit Diagrams*, place 1 dark B square atop 1 black A square, right sides facing. Stitch diagonally from corner to corner as shown. Trim ¼" beyond stitching; press open to reveal triangle. Repeat for remaining 3 corners to complete Center Unit.

Center Unit Diagrams

2. Join 1 G rectangle to top and bottom of center unit *(Round 1 Diagrams)*. Join 1 H rectangle to each side of unit. Using diagonal seams method, join 1 C square to each corner to complete round 1.

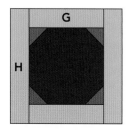

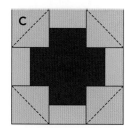

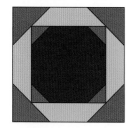

Round 1 Diagrams

3. Join 1 H rectangle to top and bottom of round 1 unit *(Round 2 Diagrams)*. Join 1 I rectangle to each side of unit. Using diagonal seams method, join 1 D square to each corner to complete round 2.

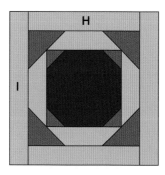

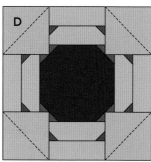

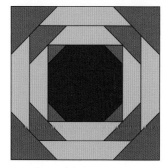

Round 2 Diagrams

4. Referring to *Pineapple Block Diagram*, continue in same manner to add rounds 3 and 4 to complete 1 Pineapple block. Make 3 Pineapple blocks.

5. Repeat steps #1–#4 using pieces listed in *Setting Block Diagrams* to complete 1 Setting block.

6. Cut Setting block in half in both directions as shown in *Setting Block Diagrams* to make 4 setting squares.

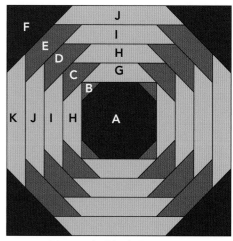

Pineapple Block Diagrams

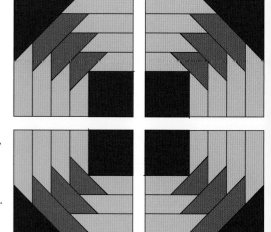

Setting Block Diagrams

Assembly Diagram

Quilt Assembly

1. Referring to *Assembly Diagram*, lay out Pineapple blocks and setting squares as shown.

2. Join into diagonal rows; join rows to complete quilt top.

Finishing

1. Layer backing, batting, and quilt top; baste. Quilt as desired. Quilt shown was quilted in the ditch around the center squares and center triangles and down the center of the light strips.

2. Join 2¼"-wide red print #1 binding strips into 1 continuous piece for straight-grain French-fold binding. Add binding to quilt.

DESIGNER

Julie Larsen enjoys using innovative methods to create traditional quilts. She owns Prairie Star Quilts in Elk Horn, Iowa. ✳

Kyoto Star

Marsha McCloskey is a master of feathered star quilts. Make this small quilt for your table or wall to show off your piecing and quilting skills.

PROJECT RATING: CHALLENGING
Size: 39½" × 39½"

MATERIALS

- ½ yard each of 4 assorted red prints for blocks, borders, and binding
- 4 fat quarters★ assorted green prints for blocks and outer border
- 4 fat quarters★ assorted light prints for background
- ½ yard each of 2 light prints for background and inner border
- 1¼ yards backing fabric
- 8" Bias Square™ Ruler (optional)
- Crib-size quilt batting
- ★fat quarter = 18" × 20"

Cutting

Measurements include ¼" seam allowances. Border strips are exact length needed. You may want to make them longer to allow for piecing variations.

NOTE: Two methods are given for cutting the pieces for the triangle-squares in this quilt. Marsha's quick method is explained in *Sew Easy: Bias-Strip Piecing* on page 125.

If you prefer, you may use traditional cutting methods. Read through all instructions before cutting.

From each red print, cut:

- 1 (8"-wide) strip. From strip, cut 1 (8") square to make 16 triangle-squares using Bias-Strip Piecing method **OR for traditional piecing, cut:** 1 (2⅛"-wide) strip. From strip, cut 8 (2⅛") squares. Cut squares in half diagonally to make 16 half-square A triangles.
- 1 (3½"-wide) strip. From strip, cut 2 (3½") squares and 1 (3⅛") I square. Cut (3½") squares in half diagonally to make 4 half-square B triangles.
- 1 (2⅛"-wide) strip. From strip, cut 4 (2⅛") squares. Cut squares in half diagonally to make 8 half-square A triangles.
- 1 (1¼"-wide) strip. From strip, cut 2 (1¼" × 16⅞") strips for middle border.

From each remaining 8"-wide red print strip, cut:

- 2 (2¼"-wide) strips for binding.

From each green print fat quarter, cut:

- 3 (3½"-wide) strips. From strips, cut 11 (3½") squares. Cut squares in half diagonally to make 22 half-square B triangles.
- 1 (1¼"-wide) strip. From strip, cut 1 (1¼") H square.

From each light print fat quarter, cut:

- 1 (8") square to make 16 triangle-squares using Bias-Strip Piecing method **OR for traditional piecing, cut:** 1 (2⅛"-wide) strip. From strip, cut 8 (2⅛") squares. Cut squares in half diagonally to make 16 half-square A triangles.

- 2 (3½"-wide) strips. From strips, cut 7 (3½") squares. Cut squares in half diagonally to make 14 half-square B triangles.
- 1 (1¾"-wide) strip. From strip, cut 9 (1¾") D squares.

From light print #1, cut:

- 1 (9¼"-wide) strip. From strip, cut 1 (9¼") F square and 4 (9¼" × 4⅞") G rectangles.
- 1 (6½"-wide) strip. From strip, cut 2 (6½") squares and 4 (4⅞") E squares. Cut 6½" squares in half diagonally in both directions to make 8 quarter-square C triangles.
- 1 (1¾"-wide) strip. From strip, cut 20 (1¾") D squares.

From light print #2, cut:

- 4 (2⅞"-wide) strips. From strips, cut 2 (2⅞" × 33¼") top and bottom inner borders and 2 (2⅞" × 28½") side inner borders.
- 1 (1¾"-wide) strip. From strip, cut 32 (1¾") D squares.

Star Point Assembly

1. Referring to *Sew Easy: Bias-Strip Piecing* on page 125, make 4 sets of 16 (1¾") triangle-squares (1¼" finished size) from 8" red print squares and 8" light print squares **OR for traditional piecing,** join 1 red print A triangle and 1 light print A triangle to make a triangle-square *(Triangle-Square Diagrams)*. Make 4 sets of 16 matching triangle-squares.

Triangle-Square Diagrams

2. Choose 1 set of 4 matching triangle-squares, 2 red print A triangles, and 1 light print D square; 1 light print #1 C triangle; and 2 matching green print B triangles. Join as shown in *Single Star Point Diagrams* to complete 1 Single Star Point. Make 8 Single Star Points.

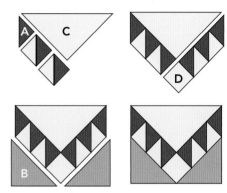

Single Star Point Diagrams

3. Choose 1 set of 8 matching triangle-squares, 4 red print A triangles, and 2 light print D squares; 2 sets of 2 matching green print B triangles; 5 light print #1 D squares; and 4 light print #2 D squares. Join as shown in *Double Star Point Diagrams* to complete 1 Double Star Point. Make 4 Double Star Points.

Pieced Border Assembly

1. Join 1 background print B triangle and 1 green print B triangle to make a triangle-square. Make 52 triangle-squares.
2. Referring to *Quilt Top Assembly Diagram*, join 13 triangle-squares as shown to make side outer border. Make 2 side outer borders.

Quilt Top Assembly Diagram

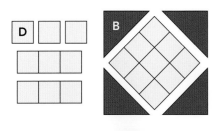

Double Star Point Diagrams

3. In the same manner, join 13 triangle-squares to make top outer border. Repeat for bottom outer border.

Quilt Assembly

1. Choose 1 matching set of 5 light print D squares and 4 matching red print B triangles; and 4 light print #2 D squares. Join as shown in *Star Center Diagrams* to make 1 Star Center. Make 4 Star Centers.

Star Center Diagrams

2. Lay out Star Centers, Single and Double Star Points, 4 light print #1 E squares, 4 G rectangles, and 1 F square as shown in *Quilt Top Assembly Diagram*. Join into rows; join rows to complete quilt center.

3. Add side inner borders to quilt center. Add top and bottom inner borders to quilt.

4. Referring to quilt center for color placement, join 2 red print border strips as shown to make 1 middle border. Make 4 middle borders.

5. Join side middle borders to quilt. Add 1 green print H square to each end of top and bottom middle borders. Add borders to quilt.

6. Add pieced side outer borders to quilt. Add 1 red print I square to each end of top and bottom outer borders. Add borders to quilt.

Finishing

1. Layer backing, batting, and quilt top; baste. Quilt as desired. Quilt shown was quilted with a curved design in the background areas and outline quilted in the triangle-squares and borders *(Quilting Diagram)*.

2. Join 2¼"-wide red print strips into 1 continuous piece for straight-grain French-fold binding. Add binding to quilt.

Quilting Diagram

DESIGNER

Marsha McCloskey teaches quiltmaking, designs quilts, writes books, and designs fabric. She lives in Eugene, Oregon, and specializes in Feathered Star designs. ✳

Bias-Strip Piecing

Make multiple 1¼"-finished triangle-squares quickly using this easy method. For instructions to make triangle-squares in other sizes, see Marsha McCloskey's book *Feathered Star Quilt Blocks I*.

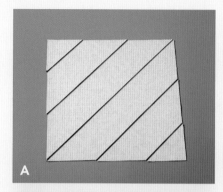

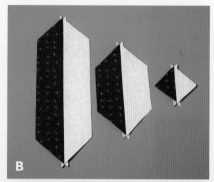

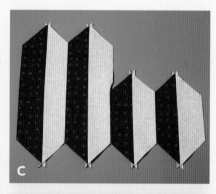

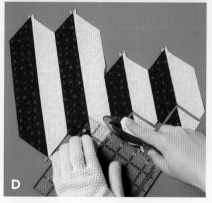

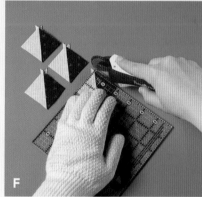

1. Place 1 (8") light square atop 1 (8") dark square, right sides facing. Cut squares in half diagonally to make 2 triangles.

2. Measuring from the long side, cut 2 (2"-wide) strips from each pair of triangles (*Photo A*). You will have 4 bias strip pairs and 2 corner triangle pairs.

3. Join bias-strip pairs and corner triangle pairs as shown in *Photo B*; press seam allowances open.

4. Join the bias strip pairs, alternating light and dark (*Photo C*). Press seam allowances open.

5. Using Bias Square™ ruler or other square ruler, cut 4 triangle-squares from the bottom of the pieced unit. Place the diagonal line of the ruler on the seam line and cut a square that is slightly larger (a few threads) than 1¾". Cut along the top edges of the ruler (*Photo D*).

Sew Smart™
To make cutting easier, use the Bias Square™ Ruler, available at www.MarshaMcCloskey.com —Liz

6. Continue cutting from the bottom edge (*Photo E*) until entire piece is cut into triangle-squares. You should get enough triangle-squares for 1 star from each pair of 8" squares.

7. Turn the squares and trim opposite sides to 1¾" (*Photo F*).

Winter

PROJECT BY **Connie Cerdena**.

Frontier Nights

Designer Connie Cerdena made this table topper as a tribute to one of her immigrant ancestors, Hans Wagner, who made a home for his family in the wilderness of western South Carolina early in the eighteenth century.

PROJECT RATING: INTERMEDIATE
Size: 42" × 42"

MATERIALS

4 fat quarters★★ assorted medium tan and brick prints for cabins

4 fat quarters★★ assorted dark red and brown prints for cabins

1 fat eighth★ red print for chimneys

1 fat eighth★ green print for center

1 fat eighth★ tan print for path

1 fat quarter★★ black solid for cabins

2 fat quarters★★ assorted gold prints for stars

¾ yard medium blue print for background

½ yard light blue print for inner border

1⅛ yards dark blue print for outer border and binding

Paper-backed fusible web

Tan and brown perle cotton

2¾ yards backing fabric

Crib-size quilt batting

★fat eighth = 9" × 20"

★★fat quarter = 18" × 20"

Cutting

Measurements include ¼" seam allowances. Patterns for Stars are on page 132. Follow manufacturer's instructions for using fusible web.

From each medium print fat quarter, cut:

- 3 (1½"-wide) strips for strip sets.

From each dark print fat quarter, cut:

- 4 (1½"-wide) strips. From 1 strip, cut 1 (1½" × 2½") A rectangle. Remaining strips are for strip sets.

From red print, cut:

- 1 (2½"-wide) strip. From strip, cut 8 (2½" × 1½") A rectangles.

From green print, cut:

- 1 (4½"-wide) strip. From strip, cut 4 (4½") F squares.

From tan print, cut:

- 2 (2½"-wide) strips. From strips, cut 1 (2½" × 10½") D rectangle, 2 (2½" × 4½") B rectangles, and 4 (2½" × 1½") A rectangles.

From black solid, cut:

- 5 (2½"-wide) strips. From strips, cut 4 (2½" × 10½") D rectangles, 4 (2½" × 4½") B rectangles, and 16 (2½" × 1½") A rectangles.

From each gold print, cut:

- 6 Small Stars.
- 2 Large Stars.

From medium blue print, cut:

- 2 (10½"-wide) strips. From strips, cut 4 (10½") G squares.

From light blue print, cut:

- 5 (2½"-wide) strips. From strips, cut 4 (2½" × 12½") H rectangles, 4 (2½" × 10½") D rectangles, and 8 (2½") E squares.

From dark blue print, cut:

- 4 (4½"-wide) strips. From strips, cut 4 (4½" × 18½") J rectangles and 4 (4½" × 14½") I rectangles.

- 2 (2½"-wide) strips. From strips, cut 4 (2½" × 6½") C rectangles and 4 (2½" × 4½") B rectangles.
- 5 (2¼"-wide) strips for binding.

Cabin Assembly

1. Referring to *Roof Unit Assembly Diagrams*, place 1 light blue E square atop 1 black D rectangle, right sides facing. Stitch diagonally from corner to corner as shown. Trim ¼" beyond stitching. Press open to reveal triangle. Repeat for opposite end of black rectangle to complete 1 Roof Unit. Make 4 Roof Units.

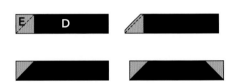

Roof Unit Assembly Diagrams

2. Join 1 medium print strip and 1 dark print strip as shown in *Strip Set Diagram*. Make 4 sets of 3 matching strip sets. From each set of strip sets, cut 6 (4½"-wide) segments, 6 (2½"-wide) segments, and 4 (1½"-wide) segments.

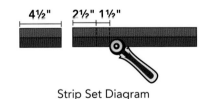

Strip Set Diagram

3. Lay out 1 Roof Unit, matching strip set segments and dark print A rectangle, 4 black A rectangles, 1 black B rectangle, and 1 tan print A rectangle as shown in *Cabin Assembly Diagram*. Join pieces to complete 1 Cabin (*Cabin Diagram*). Make 4 Cabins.

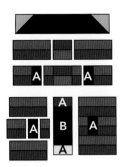

Cabin Assembly Diagram

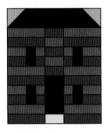

Cabin Diagram

Center Path Unit Assembly

1. Lay out 4 green print F squares, 1 tan print D rectangle, and 2 tan print B rectangles as shown in *Center Path Unit Assembly Diagram*.

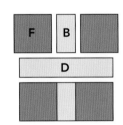

Center Path Unit Assembly Diagram

2. Join pieces as shown in *Center Path Unit Diagram*.

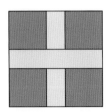

Center Path Unit Diagram

Corner Unit Assembly

1. Lay out 1 medium blue G square, 1 light blue D rectangle, and 1 light blue H rectangle as shown in *Corner Unit Assembly Diagram.*

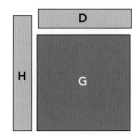

Corner Unit Assembly Diagram

2. Join pieces to complete 1 Corner Unit *(Corner Unit Diagram)*. Make 4 Corner Units.

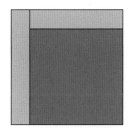

Corner Unit Diagram

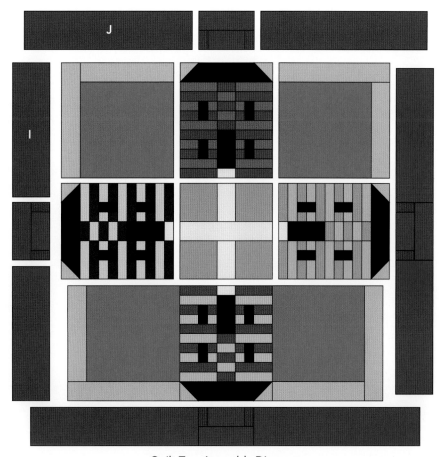

Quilt Top Assembly Diagram

Quilt Assembly

1. Lay out Cabins, Center Path Unit, and Corner Units as shown in *Quilt Top Assembly Diagram.* Join into rows; join rows to complete quilt center.

2. Referring to *Chimney Unit Assembly Diagrams*, join 1 dark blue print B rectangle, 2 dark red print A rectangles, and 1 dark blue print C rectangle as shown to make 1 Chimney Unit. Make 4 Chimney Units.

Chimney Unit Assembly Diagrams

3. Join 1 Chimney Unit and 2 dark blue print I rectangles as shown in *Quilt Top Assembly Diagram* to make 1 side outer border. Make 2 side outer borders. Join to sides of quilt center.

4. Join 1 Chimney Unit and 2 dark blue print J rectangles to make top outer border. Repeat for bottom outer border. Add top and bottom borders to quilt.

5. Referring to photo on page 133, fuse stars to quilt top. Blanket stitch around stars using brown perle cotton *(Stitch Diagrams)*.

6. Chain stitch "smoke" rising from chimneys using tan perle cotton *(Stitch Diagrams)*.

STITCH DIAGRAMS

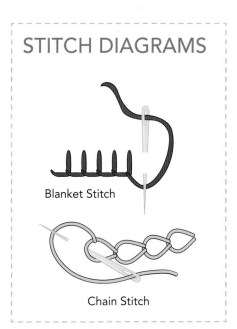

Blanket Stitch

Chain Stitch

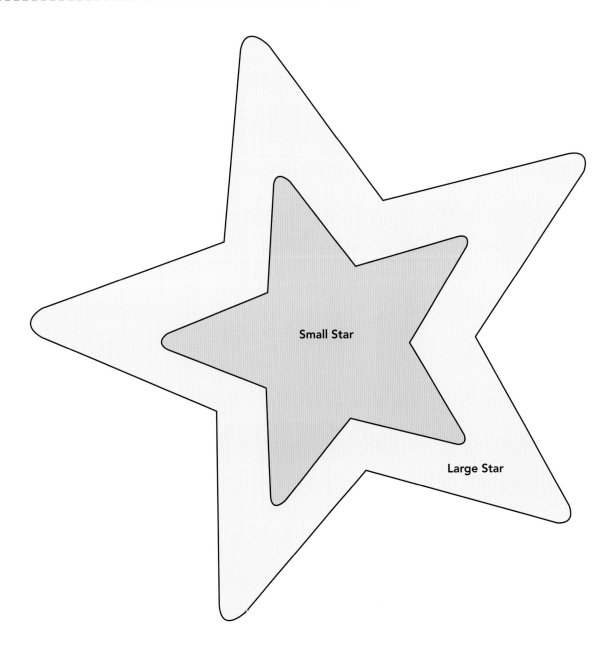

Small Star

Large Star

Finishing

1. Divide backing into 2 (1⅜-yard) lengths. Cut 1 piece in half lengthwise to make 2 narrow panels. Join 1 narrow panel to wider panel. Remaining panel is extra and can be used to make a hanging sleeve.

2. Layer backing, batting, and quilt top; baste. Quilt as desired. Quilt shown was quilted in the ditch in the cabins and around stars, with a cable in the paths, and with a diagonal grid in the corner units and outer borders. *(Quilting Diagram)*.

3. Join 2¼"-wide dark blue print strips into 1 continuous piece for straight-grain French-fold binding. Add binding to quilt.

Quilting Diagram

DESIGNER

Connie Cerdena has been creating quilts for over thirty years, many of them sold at shows or as commissioned works. She has made many traditional quilts, but her true passion is creating small appliquéd quilts. Connie turned this passion into a quilt and cross-stitch pattern company, Jenny Creek Designs. ✳

TRIED & TRUE

We used prints from Windham Fabrics' Software collection by Yolanda Fundora with Barbara Campbell to make a bright, fun block.

Reindeer
Table Runner

This lovely wool table runner may become your all-time favorite holiday decoration. The shapes are simple and quick to stitch.

PROJECT RATING: EASY

Size: 12" × 42½"

MATERIALS

1 yard tan felted wool

¼ yard red felted wool

⅛ yard dark green felted wool

Freezer paper

#8 Perle cotton in green and light gold

Cutting

Make freezer paper templates from patterns on page 136. Press templates onto wool and cut out shapes from desired fabrics; remove paper.

From tan wool, cut:

• 2 (12" × 36") rectangles.

• 8 Large Tongues.

From red wool, cut:

• 7 Reindeer.

• 8 Small Tongues.

• 14 Small Circles.

From dark green wool, cut:

• 8 Medium Tongues.

• 14 Large Circles.

Table Runner Assembly

NOTE: See Sew Easy: Decorative Embroidery Stitches on page 137 for instructions for all stitches used in this project.

1. Referring to *Assembly Diagram*, place 1 red Small Tongue atop 1 dark green Medium Tongue. Blanket stitch in place using green perle cotton. In the same manner, using light gold perle cotton, blanket stitch green Medium Tongue to tan Large Tongue. Using green perle cotton, blanket stitch around curved outer edge of tan Large Tongue. Make 8 tongues.

2. Center 1 red Small Circle atop 1 green Large Circle. Stitch in place using light gold perle cotton and spoke stitch.

3. Referring to photo on page 134 and *Assembly Diagram*, lay out reindeer and circles on 1 tan background rectangle. Using matching regular sewing thread, whipstitch reindeer to background. Using gold perle cotton, blanket stitch circles to background.

4. Position tongues on ends of background rectangle as shown, with ¼" of each tongue extending under the background piece. Pin or baste in place.

5. Position remaining tan rectangle on back side of runner, aligning it with front background rectangle. Using tan thread, whipstitch backing in place, securing tongues and backing to front

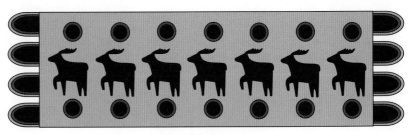

Assembly Diagram

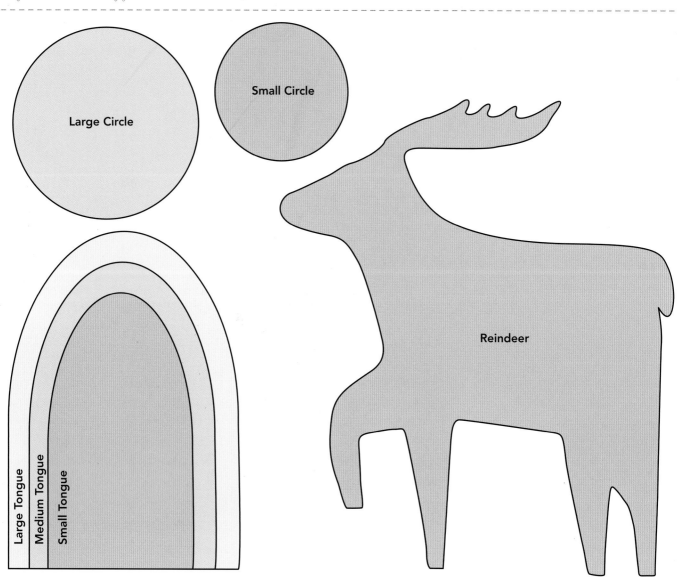

Large Circle

Small Circle

Reindeer

Large Tongue

Medium Tongue

Small Tongue

background rectangle. Using green perle cotton, blanket stitch around the outer edges of background rectangle.

DESIGNER

Jan Speed began designing patterns several years ago, focusing primarily on wool and embroidery patterns. Jan also enjoys painting and drawing. ✳

TRIED & TRUE

Reverse the colors for a totally different look. We made our smaller version with light reindeer on a dark background. Red background panel is 12" × 18".

Sew Easy™
Decorative Embroidery Stitches

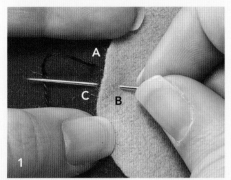 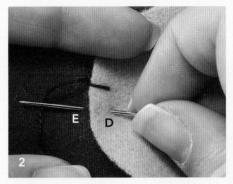 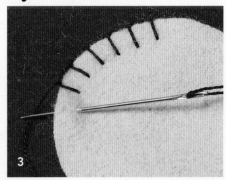

Blanket Stitch:

1. Bring needle to right side of fabric at A, just outside the edge of the appliqué piece. Insert needle at B and bring it up at C, over the thread. Pull thread taut so stitch lies flat, but not tight enough to pucker fabric. **2.** Insert needle at D and bring it up at E, over the thread. **3.** Continue in this manner. Secure last stitch with a tiny stitch to anchor the loop.

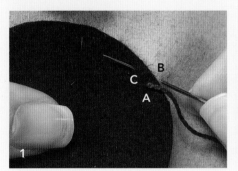 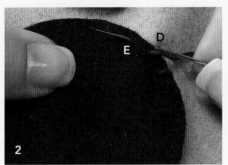 

Whipstitch:

1. Bring needle to right side of fabric at A, through background and appliqué piece. Insert needle at B, just outside the edge of the appliqué piece. Bring needle to right side at C through background and appliqué piece. **2.** Insert needle at D and bring it up at E. **3.** Continue in this manner. Secure thread on back side by making a shallow knot.

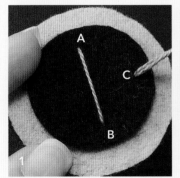  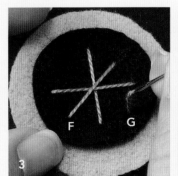 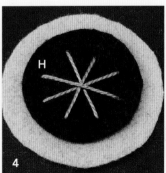

Spoke Stitch:

1. Bring needle to right side of fabric at A. Insert needle at B and bring it up at C. Pull thread until stitch lies flat, but not tight enough to pucker fabric. **2.** Insert needle at D and bring it up at E. **3.** Insert needle at F and bring it up at G. **4.** Insert needle at H. Secure thread on back side by making a shallow knot.

Liberty Star

Shon McMain liked this block so well when she made samples for a "Quilting with Fons & Porter" TV program, that she joined three of them into a festive table runner to use during the holiday season.

PROJECT RATING: CHALLENGING
Size: 14½" × 49½"

MATERIALS

¼ yard each red, green, and gold prints for stars
1 yard cream print for background and binding
1½ yards backing fabric
20" × 55" rectangle quilt batting
Freezer paper

Cutting

Measurements include ¼" seam allowances.

From each red, green, and gold print, cut:

• 4 (1½"-wide) strips for strip sets.

From cream print, cut:

• 1 (7¼"-wide) strip. From strip, cut 3 (7¼") squares. Cut squares in half diagonally in both directions to make 12 quarter-square A triangles.
  (2 are extra.)

• 2 (4¾"-wide) strips. From strips, cut 4 (4¾") B squares and 4 (4¾" × 9") C rectangles.

• 4 (2¼"-wide) strips for binding.

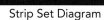

Strip Set Diagram

Star Assembly

NOTE: Refer to *Sew Easy: Quick Cutting 45-degree Diamonds* on page 143 for photos and tips on cutting diamonds from a strip set.

1. Join 1 red, 1 gold, and 1 green strip, offsetting strips by approximately 1" as shown in *Strip Set Diagram*. Make 4 strip sets.

2. Using 45-degree angle line on ruler as a guide, trim end of strip set at 45-degree angle. To cut a 45-degree diamond, make a second cut parallel to the first cut and 3½" away. Cut 24 diamonds from strip sets.

3. Cut 6 (3" × 18") strips from freezer paper. Using 45-degree angle on ruler as a guide, trim 1 end of each paper strip at a 45-degree angle. To cut a 45-degree diamond, make a second cut parallel to the first cut and 3" away. Cut 24 paper diamonds.

4. Center and press shiny side of 1 paper diamond to wrong side of 1 fabric diamond to stabilize fabric diamond. Repeat for all diamonds.

5. Lay out 8 diamonds to form a star as shown in *Variation 1 Diagram* or *Variation 2 Diagram*. Diamonds in table runner are arranged with red strips to the center.

Variation 1 Diagram

Variation 2 Diagram

6. Referring to *Star Assembly Diagram*, join 4 diamonds to form a half star. Backstitch beginning and ends of seams. Start and stop stitching at corners of paper diamonds so seam allowances (ends of fabric diamonds) are free.

Sew Smart™

Leaving the ends free helps prevent a lumpy center and allows for setting triangles and squares into the outside of the star. —Liz

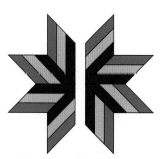

Star Assembly Diagram

7. Repeat to make a second half star. Join star halves to complete 1 star *(Star Diagram)*. Make 3 stars.

Star Diagram

Quilt Assembly

1. Lay out stars and cream A, B, and C pieces as shown in *Quilt Top Assembly Diagram*.

2. Beginning with the star on the left, set 1 cream A triangle into opening at top of star. Stitch from outside of star toward the inside, stopping stitching and backstitching ¼" from inner corner (edge of freezer paper). Repeat to join adjacent side of triangle to star.

3. Set 3 additional triangles into star as shown.

4. Set 1 B square into left edge of star.

5. In the same manner, set 4 A triangles and 1 B square into star at right end of table runner.

6. Set A triangles into center star.

7. Join left star and center star by setting in 1 B square and 2 C rectangles as shown. In the same manner, add right star to opposite side of center star to complete the table runner top. Remove freezer paper backing from diamonds.

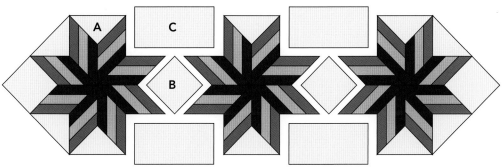

Quilt Top Assembly Diagram

Finishing

1. Cut backing fabric in half lengthwise to make two narrow panels. 1 panel is extra.

2. Layer quilt top, batting, and backing; baste. Quilt as desired. Table runner was quilted ¼" to inside of red strips with a fleur-de-lis design quilted in the cream triangles, squares, and rectangles *(Quilting Diagram)*.

3. Join 2¼"-wide cream strips into 1 continuous piece for French-fold binding. Add binding to quilt.

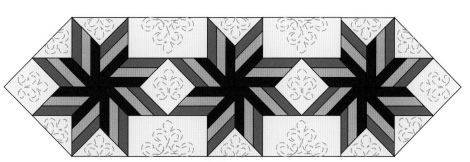

Quilting Diagram

Fleur-de-lis Quilting Pattern

DESIGNER

Whether she's choosing fabrics, creating original designs, piecing, or quilting, Shon McMain loves every aspect of making quilts. Her designs have appeared in many issues of *Love of Quilting*. She lives in West Des Moines, Iowa. ✻

TRIED & TRUE

A traditional patriotic red, white, and blue color scheme was used for this Liberty Star block.

Sew Easy™

Quick Cutting 45-degree Diamonds

We used a rotary cutter and ruler with 45-degree angle markings to quick cut the diamonds for our *Liberty Star* holiday table runner on page 138. You can use this quick and easy method to cut diamonds from a strip set, as we did, or to cut them from a single fabric strip. Just follow these simple steps.

Supplies

Rotary cutting ruler with 45-degree angle cutting guidelines

Instructions

1. Measure the width of your strip set or strip. Ours is 3½" wide (*Photo A*).
2. Using the 45-degree angle line on your ruler as a guide, trim one end of the strip set at a 45-degree angle (*Photo B*).
3. Position ruler atop strip set so the cutting guideline that corresponds with your strip width (3½" guide for this sample) is along the angled edge of strip and the 45-degree angle line on ruler is atop the long top or bottom edge of the strip. Cut along the edge of the ruler (*Photo C*).
4. In this manner, continue cutting until you have 8 diamonds for a star (*Photo D*).
5. To check the accuracy of your diamonds, fold diamond in half across the larger angle (*Photo E*). The tips of the diamonds will meet if you have cut a true diamond.

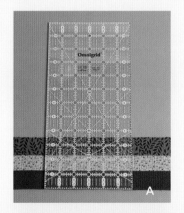

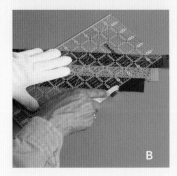
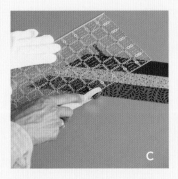
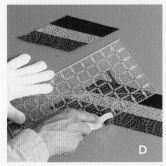

PROJECT DESIGNED BY **Gudrun Erla**.
MADE BY **Yvonne Geske**.
MACHINE QUILTED BY **Rita Kroening**.

Holiday Cheer

With its woodsy look, this quilt is perfect for a holiday table or to hang above a fireplace.

PROJECT RATING: INTERMEDIATE

Size: 47" × 47"

Blocks: 5 (6") Star blocks

MATERIALS

1¼ yards light gold print

¾ yard medium gold print

⅜ yard dark gold print

¼ yard brown print

¼ yard light green print

¼ yard medium green print

⅜ yard dark green print

1½ yards rust print for borders and binding

Paper-backed fusible web

Fons & Porter Half & Quarter Ruler (optional)

3 yards backing fabric

Twin-size quilt batting

Cutting

Measurements include ¼" seam allowances. Border strips are exact length needed. You may want to make them longer to allow for piecing variations. Patterns for Holly Leaf and Berry are on page 149. Follow manufacturer's instructions for using fusible web. For instructions on using the Fons & Porter Half & Quarter Ruler, go to www.FonsandPorter.com/sehfquart.

> ### Sew **Smart**™
> To cut half-square C triangles and quarter-square D triangles from the same width strip, use the Fons & Porter Half & Quarter Ruler. If you are not using the Fons & Porter Half & Quarter Ruler, use the cutting NOTE instructions given here.   —Marianne

From light gold print, cut:

- 3 (4"-wide) strips. From strips, cut 24 (4") P squares.

- 3 (3"-wide) strips. From strips, cut 8 (3" × 7½") Q rectangles and 8 (3") M squares.

- 4 (2½"-wide) strips. From strips, cut 16 (2½" × 3") L rectangles, and 32 (2½") K squares.

- 4 (2"-wide) strips. From strips, cut 24 (2") B squares, 16 half-square C triangles, and 24 quarter-square D triangles.

NOTE: If NOT using the Fons & Porter Half & Quarter Ruler to cut the C triangles, cut 1 (2⅜"-wide) strip. From strip, cut 8 (2⅜") squares. Cut squares in half diagonally to make 16 half-square C triangles.

NOTE: If NOT using the Fons & Porter Half & Quarter Ruler to cut the D triangles, cut 1 (4¼"-wide) strip. From strip, cut 6 (4¼") squares. Cut squares in half diagonally in both directions to make 24 quarter-square D triangles.

From medium gold print, cut:

- 1 (9⅜"-wide) strip. From strip, cut 2 (9⅜") squares. Cut squares in half diagonally to make 4 half-square F triangles.
- 3 (3½"-wide) strips. From strips, cut 4 (3½" × 10½") J rectangles and 4 (3½" × 7½") I rectangles.
- 2 (1½"-wide) strips. From strips, cut 4 (1½" × 7½") H rectangles and 4 (1½" × 6½") G rectangles.

From dark gold print, cut:

- 1 (3½"-wide) strip. From strip, cut 5 (3½") A squares.
- 1 (2"-wide) strip. From strip cut 4 (2") B squares and 4 quarter-square D triangles.

  NOTE: If NOT using the Fons & Porter Half & Quarter Ruler to cut the D triangles, cut 1 (4¼"-wide) strip. From strip cut 1 (4¼") square. Cut square in half diagonally in both directions to make 4 quarter-square D triangles.

From brown print, cut:

- 1 (2½"-wide) strip. From strip, cut 4 (2½" × 3") L rectangles and 8 (2½") K squares.
- 1 (2"-wide) strip. From strip, cut 16 half-square C triangles.

NOTE: If NOT using the Fons & Porter Half & Quarter Ruler to cut the C triangles, cut 1 (2⅜"-wide) strip. From strip, cut 8 (2⅜") squares. Cut squares in half diagonally to make 16 half-square C triangles.

From light green print, cut:

- 1 (7½"-wide) strip. From strip, cut 4 (7½" × 4") O rectangles and 5 (7½" × 2½") N rectangles.

From medium green print, cut:

- 1 (7½"-wide) strip. From strip, cut 4 (7½" × 4") O rectangles and 5 (7½" × 2½") N rectangles.

From dark green print, cut:

- 1 (7½"-wide) strip. From strip, cut 4 (7½" × 4") O rectangles and 6 (7½" × 2½") N rectangles.
- 8 Holly Leaves.

From rust print, cut:

- 1 (3⅞"-wide) strip. From strip, cut 4 (3⅞") squares. Cut squares in half diagonally to make 8 half-square E triangles.
- 5 (3½"-wide) strips. Piece strips to make 2 (3½" × 47½") top and bottom outer borders and 2 (3½" × 41½") side outer borders.
- 3 (2½"-wide) strips. From strips, cut 2 (2½" × 21½") top and bottom inner borders and 2 (2½" × 17½") side inner borders.
- 6 (2¼"-wide) strips for binding.
- 2 (2"-wide) strips. From strips, cut 40 half-square C triangles.

  NOTE: If NOT using the Fons & Porter Half & Quarter Ruler to cut the C triangles, cut 2 (2⅜"-wide) strips. From strips, cut 20 (2⅜") squares. Cut squares in half diagonally to make 40 half-square C triangles.

- 12 Holly Berries.

Block Assembly

1. Lay out 1 light gold print D triangle and 2 rust print C triangles as shown in *Flying Geese Unit Diagrams*. Join triangles to complete 1 Flying Geese Unit. Make 20 rust Flying Geese Units.

Flying Geese Unit Diagrams

2. In the same manner, make 4 brown Flying Geese Units using light gold print D triangles and brown print C triangles.

3. Lay out 4 rust Flying Geese Units, 4 light gold print B squares, and 1 dark gold A square as shown in *Block Assembly Diagram*. Join into rows; join rows to complete 1 Star block *(Block Diagram)*. Make 5 Star blocks.

Block Assembly Diagram

Block Diagram

Center Assembly

1. Lay out 1 brown Flying Geese Unit, 2 light gold print C triangles, 1 dark gold print D triangle, and 2 rust print E triangles as shown in *Side Unit Diagrams*. Join to complete 1 Side Unit. Make 4 Side Units.

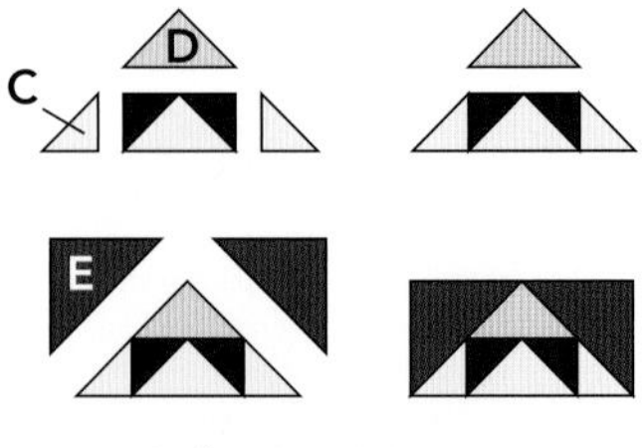

Side Unit Diagrams

2. Join 1 light gold C triangle and 1 brown print C triangle as shown in *Triangle-Square Diagrams*. Make 8 triangle-squares.

Triangle-Square Diagrams

3. Lay out 2 triangle-squares, 1 light gold print B square, and 1 dark gold print B square as shown in *Corner Unit Diagrams*. Join into rows; join rows to complete 1 Corner Unit. Make 4 Corner Units.

Corner Unit Diagrams

4. Lay out 4 Corner Units, 4 Side Units, and 1 Star block as shown in *Center Unit Diagrams*. Join into rows; join rows to complete Center Unit.

Center Unit Diagrams

Tree Unit Assembly

1. Referring to *Diagonal Seams Unit Diagrams*, place 1 light gold print K square atop 1 assorted green print N rectangle, right sides facing. Stitch diagonally from corner to corner as

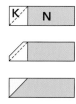

Diagonal Seams Unit Diagrams

shown. Trim ¼" beyond stitching. Press open to reveal triangle to complete 1 Diagonal Seams Unit. Make 16 Diagonal Seams Units.

2. In the same manner, make 12 Tree Top Units using light gold print P squares and assorted green print O rectangles *(Tree Top Unit Diagram)*.

Tree Top Unit Diagram

3. Lay out 1 Diagonal Seams Unit, 1 Tree Top Unit, 1 brown print K square, 2 light gold print L rectangles, and 1 light gold print Q rectangle as shown in *Short Tree Unit Diagrams*. Join into sections; join sections to complete 1 Short Tree Unit. Make 8 Short Tree Units.

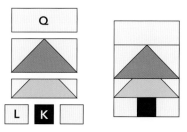

Short Tree Unit Diagrams

4. Lay out 2 Diagonal Seams Units, 1 Tree Top Unit, 1 brown print L rectangle, and 2 light gold print M squares as shown in *Tall Tree Unit Diagrams*. Join into sections; join sections to complete 1 Tall Tree Unit. Make 4 Tall Tree Units.

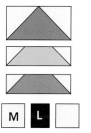 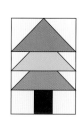

Tall Tree Unit Diagrams

Pieced Border Assembly

1. Lay out 1 Star Block, 1 medium gold print G rectangle, 1 medium gold print H rectangle, 1 medium gold print I rectangle, and 1 medium gold print J rectangle as shown in *Border Corner Unit Diagrams*. Join to complete 1 Border Corner Unit background.

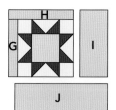

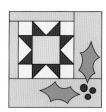

Border Corner Unit Diagrams

2. Position 2 Holly Leaves and 3 Holly Berries atop 1 Border Corner Unit background as shown. Machine appliqué using matching thread to complete 1 Border Corner Unit. Make 4 Border Corner Units.

3. Lay out 2 Short Tree Units and 1 Tall Tree Unit as shown in *Quilt Top Assembly Diagram* on page 148. Join to make 1 pieced border. Make 4 pieced borders.

Quilt Top Assembly Diagram

Quilt Assembly

1. Lay out Center Unit and 4 medium gold print F triangles as shown in *Quilt Top Assembly Diagram*. Join to complete quilt center.

2. Add rust print side inner borders to quilt center. Add rust print top and bottom inner borders to quilt.

3. Referring to *Quilt Top Assembly Diagram*, add pieced borders to sides of quilt.

4. Add 1 Border Corner Unit to each end of remaining pieced borders. Add borders to top and bottom of quilt.

5. Add rust print side outer borders to quilt center. Add rust print top and bottom outer borders to quilt.

Finishing

1. Divide backing into 2 (1½-yard) lengths. Cut 1 piece in half lengthwise to make 2 narrow panels. Join 1 narrow panel to wider panel. Remaining panel is extra and can be used to make a hanging sleeve.

2. Layer backing, batting, and quilt top; baste. Quilt as desired. Quilt shown was quilted in the ditch, with holly leaf and berry designs, and meandering in background areas *(Quilting Diagram)*.

3. Join 2¼"-wide rust print strips into 1 continuous piece for straight-grain French-fold binding. Add binding to quilt.

Quilting Diagram

DESIGNER

Gudrun Erla was born and raised in Iceland, and moved to Minnesota in 2003. She has published over 45 patterns and six books, and has designed several fabric collections for Red Rooster Fabrics. ✳

TRIED & TRUE

Substitute graphic black-and-white prints and bright colors as we did. Fabrics shown are from the Luna collection by Gail Fountain and Maywood Studio.

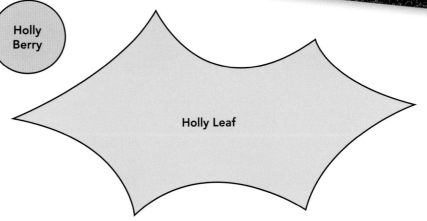

Holly Berry

Holly Leaf

Hexagon Star

Kaye Wood's Hexagon Star project is a great beginner project since there are no points to match. The center of the star is a perfect place to feature a large fabric motif such as the flower on the star shown at left. See *Sew Easy: Making Hexagon Stars* on page 153 to learn Kaye's techniques to make this project go together quickly.

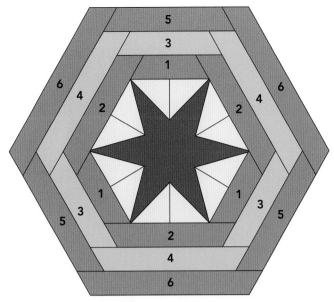

Quilt Top Assembly Diagram

PROJECT RATING: EASY
Size: 15" × 17"

MATERIALS

1 fat eighth★ red large-scale floral print for center hexagon
1 fat quarter★★ cream print for triangles
¾ yard red print for inner and outer borders and backing
1 fat eighth★ light green print for middle border
View & Do™ Hexagons or template material
★fat eighth = 9" × 20"
★★fat quarter = 18" × 20"

Cutting

If you are not using Kaye's View & Do™ Hexagons, make a template from the hexagon pattern on page 152. Measurements include ¼" seam allowances.

From red large-scale floral print, cut:
• 1 (8") center hexagon using View & Do™ Hexagon or hexagon template. If desired, fussy cut to center a motif in the hexagon.

From cream print, cut:
• 2 (4¾"-wide) strips for folded triangles. Press strips in half lengthwise. From folded strips, cut 6 (4¾"-wide) segments.

From red print, cut:
• 1 (18") square for backing.
• 3 (1¾"-wide) strips. From strips, cut 3 (1¾" × 11") #6 border strips, 3 (1¾" × 8") #5 border strips, 3 (1¾" × 8") #2 border strips, and 3 (1¾" × 5") #1 border strips.

From light green print, cut:
• 3 (1¾"-wide) strips. From strips, cut 3 (1¾" × 9½") #4 border strips and 3 (1¾" × 6½") #3 border strips.

Quilt Assembly

Note: Refer to *Sew Easy: Making Hexagon Stars* on page 153 for detailed instructions on this technique.

1. Assemble center hexagon star.
2. Referring to *Quilt Top Assembly Diagram*, add #1 border strips to center. Trim ends of strips even with center hexagon.
3. In the same manner, add #2 border strips and trim ends. Continue adding border strips in numerical order, trimming after each set is added.

Finishing

1. Cut backing ¾" larger than quilt top on all sides.
2. Place backing, wrong side up; center quilt top, right side up, atop backing. (Quilt shown has no batting and is not quilted.)
3. Fold 1 edge of backing fabric to the front, lining up the edge of the backing with the edge of quilt top; press. Repeat for remaining edges.
4. Fold each side of backing to front again and press. Pin in place.
5. Topstitch along the fold, using a straight or decorative stitch.

DESIGNER

A self-described quilt engineer with a degree in business education and math, Kaye Wood has designed quilting tools to make quilters' lives easier. These tools include the View & Do™ Shapes used for her *Hexagon Star* table topper. She also designs strip piecing techniques that simplify the cutting and sewing process. Kaye is well-known for hosting many seasons of "Kaye's Quilting Friends" on public television. ✳

TRIED & TRUE

We used a sports print for the center hexagon and added only two borders to make a smaller table mat.

Fold

½ Hexagon

Fold

Sew Easy™

Making Hexagon Stars
by Kaye Wood

Create exciting dimensional stars with no-problem points using my quick and easy technique. Start with a fussy-cut hexagon and place folded triangles atop it to create the star shape. The View & Do™ Hexagon Shape makes centering a motif in the hexagon easy.

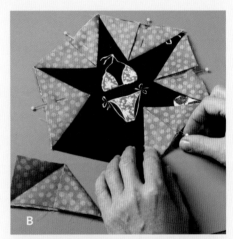

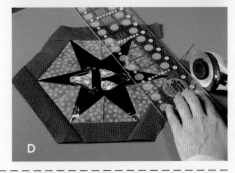

1. Using the 8" View & Do™ Hexagon or a template made from the pattern on page 152, center a motif in the hexagon (Photo A). Cut out hexagon.

2. Fold the hexagon in half to find the center of each side; place a pin on each side to mark center.

3. Fold strip for center triangles in half lengthwise, wrong sides together. Baste ⅛" from raw edges. Cut strip into 4¾" segments. Fold each segment into a triangle by bringing the outside corners from the fold down to the center bottom; press (Photo B).

4. Center and pin 1 folded triangle on each side of center hexagon. The raw edges of the triangles and center hexagon will be even. Baste ⅛" from raw edges.

5. Add #1 border strips to 3 sides of hexagon. Press seam allowances toward border strips. Trim border strips even with edge of hexagon (Photo C).

6. Add #2 border strips to 3 sides of hexagon. Press seam allowances toward border strips. Trim border strips even with edge of hexagon (Photo D).

7. Continue adding border strips in numerical order, trimming after each set.

Java Jive

Rhonda Richards' love of coffee inspired her to make this cheerful quilt from bright fabrics. She used the right side of the printed fabrics for the cups, and the wrong side of the prints for the interiors of the cups. This design makes a fun table topper for a kitchen table.

PROJECT RATING: EASY

Size: 54" × 72"

Blocks: 48 (9") Coffee Cup blocks

MATERIALS

24 fat quarters★ assorted bright prints
½ yard green print for binding
Paper-backed fusible web
3½ yards backing fabric
Twin-size quilt batting
★fat quarter = 18" × 20"

Cutting

Measurements include ¼" seam allowances. Pattern for cup is on page 156. Follow manufacturer's instructions for using fusible web. Refer to *Sew Easy: Windowing Fusible Appliqué* on page 157.

From each fat quarter, cut:

- 2 (9½") squares.
- 2 Cups.
- 2 Insides. Note: fabric is wrong side up on these pieces.

From green print, cut:

- 7 (2¼"-wide) strips for binding.

Block Assembly

1. Referring to *Block Diagram*, arrange 1 Cup and 1 Inside on 1 bright background square. Fuse pieces in place.

Block Diagram

2. Using contrasting thread, machine blanket stitch around Cup and Inside piece to complete 1 block.

4. Make 48 blocks.

Quilt Assembly

1. Referring to photograph on page 155, lay out blocks in 8 horizontal rows of 6 blocks each.

2. Join into rows; join rows to complete quilt top.

Finishing

1. Divide backing fabric into 2 (1¾-yard) lengths. Cut 1 piece in half lengthwise to make 2 narrow panels. Join 1 narrow panel to each side of wide panel; press seam allowances toward narrow panels. Seams will run horizontally.

2. Layer backing, batting, and quilt top; baste. Quilt as desired. Quilt shown was quilted with curls of steam rising from each cup.

3. Join 2¼"-wide green print strips into 1 continuous piece for straight-grain French-fold binding. Add binding to quilt.

Inside

Cup

Patterns are shown full size and are reversed for use with fusible web. Add ³⁄₁₆" seam allowance for hand appliqué.

DESIGNER

Rhonda Richards, former managing editor of *Love of Quilting,* is a prolific quilter who likes to experiment with new designs and techniques. ✳

Sew Easy™

Windowing Fusible Appliqué

Choose a lightweight "sewable" fusible product. The staff at your favorite quilt shop can recommend brands. Always read and follow manufacturer's instructions for proper fusing time and iron temperature.

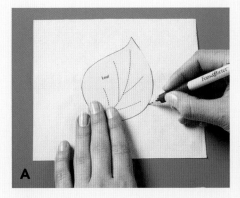

A

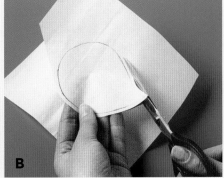

B

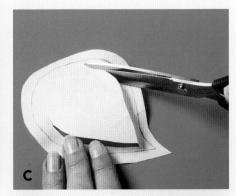

C

Sew Smart™

Fused shapes will be the reverse of the pattern you trace. If it's important for an object to face a certain direction, make a reverse pattern to trace. We do this quickly by tracing the design on tracing paper, then turning the paper over and tracing the design through onto the other side of the paper. —Liz

1. Trace appliqué motifs onto paper side of fusible web, making a separate tracing for each appliqué needed (*Photo A*).

2. Roughly cut out drawn appliqué shapes, cutting about ¼" outside drawn lines (*Photo B*).

3. "Window" fusible by trimming out the interior of the shape, leaving a scant ¼" inside drawn line (*Photo C*). Follow manufacturer's instructions to fuse web

side of each shape to wrong side of appliqué fabric.

4. Cut out appliqués, cutting carefully on drawn outline (*Photo D*). Only a thin band of fusible web frames the shape.

5. Peel off paper backing (*Photo E*). Position appliqué in place on background fabric, and follow manufacturer's instructions to fuse shapes in place.

Sew Smart™

If you have trouble peeling the paper backing, try scoring paper with a pin to give you an edge to begin with. —Marianne

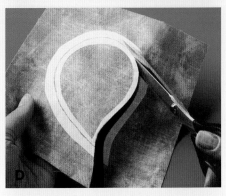

D

E

Rita's Espresso Yourself

Marianne Fons made this peppy wall quilt for the owner of her favorite coffee shop. She used rubber stamps and permanent ink to stamp Rita's name and the name of the shop on the cups. This quilt is the perfect size to place on a small table to share a cup of coffee with a friend.

PROJECT RATING: EASY

Size: 24" × 24"

Blocks: 4 (9") Coffee Cup blocks

MATERIALS

⅜ yard tan print #1 for block backgrounds

⅜ yard tan print #2 for sashing strips

1 fat eighth★ each red, green, blue, and purple prints for cups, sashing squares, and binding

1 fat eighth★ cream print for cup inside pieces

½ yard fusible web

1 yard backing fabric

Cream perle cotton (optional)

27" square quilt batting

★fat eighth = 9" × 20"

Cutting

Measurements include ¼" seam allowances. Pattern for cup is on page 156. Follow manufacturer's instructions for using fusible web. Refer to *Sew Easy: Windowing Fusible Appliqué* on page 157.

From tan print #1, cut:
• 1 (9½"-wide) strip. From strip, cut 4 (9½") squares.

From tan print #2, cut:
• 3 (2½"-wide) strips. From strips, cut 12 (2½" × 9½") sashing rectangles.

From each red, green, blue, and purple prints, cut:
• 1 Cup.
• 3 (2½") sashing squares.
• 1–2 (2¼" × 20") strips for scrappy binding.

From cream print fat eighth, cut:
• 4 Insides.

Block Assembly

1. Referring to *Block Diagram* on page 154, arrange 1 Cup and 1 Inside on 1 background square. Fuse pieces in place.

2. Machine blanket stitch around Cup and Inside piece to complete 1 block. Make 4 blocks.

Quilt Assembly

1. Referring to photograph on page 159, lay out blocks, sashing strips, and sashing squares.

2. Join into rows; join rows to complete quilt top.

Finishing

1. Layer backing, batting, and quilt top; baste. Quilt as desired. Quilt shown was outline quilted around cup shapes and along sashing and sashing squares. If desired, make long running stitches with perle cotton to embroider 3 lines of steam rising from each cup.

2. Join assorted color binding strips to make approximately 110" of straight-grain French-fold binding. Add binding to quilt.

Crazy Hearts

This quilt is fun to make for Valentine's Day from a collection of red fabrics.
If you love hearts like designer Lyndsay Sharratt does, make it with fabric scraps and
use it year round as a topper for an accent table.

PROJECT RATING: EASY

Size: 33¼" × 33¼" including
Prairie Points

Blocks: 4 (9") Heart blocks

MATERIALS

¾ yard white print for background
and border

8 fat quarters★ assorted red prints
for hearts, inner borders, and
prairie points

Paper-backed fusible web

1 yard backing fabric

35" square quilt batting

★fat quarter = 18" × 20"

Note: See *Sew Easy: Prairie Point Edging*
on page 163 for instructions on finishing
your quilt with prairie points.

Cutting

Measurements include ¼" seam
allowances. Pattern for Heart is on page
162. Follow manufacturer's instructions
for using fusible web.

From white, cut:

• 1 (9½"-wide) strip. From strip, cut
4 (9½") squares.

• 4 (3"-wide) strips. From strips, cut
2 (3" × 25") side outer borders,
2 (3" × 30") top and bottom outer
borders, and 4 (3") corner squares.

From each red print fat quarter, cut:

• 1 (4¼"-wide) strip. From strip, cut
4 (4¼") squares for prairie points.

• 2 (2"-wide) strips for border and
sashing strip sets.

• 2–3 assorted strips, ranging from
¾"–2" wide for strip sets.

From remainder of red prints, cut:

• 4 (2" × 3") rectangles for inner
borders.

• 1 (2") square for quilt center.

Block Assembly

1. Join assorted width red strips to
make strip set at least 7" wide. (You
may need to cut additional red strips,
depending on the width of strips you
originally cut.) Make 2 strip sets.

2. From strip sets cut 4 Hearts.

3. Position 1 Heart atop background
square; fuse in place. Machine or hand
blanket stitch around Heart to complete
1 Heart block. Make 4 Heart blocks.

Quilt Assembly

**Refer to photograph on page 160 to
assemble quilt top.**

1. Join 6 (2"-wide) red strips to make
strip set. Make 2 strip sets.

2. From strip sets, cut 4 (2"-wide)
segments for sashing and 8 (3"-wide)
segments for inner borders.

3. Lay out 4 Heart blocks, 4 (2"-wide)
red sashing segments, and 1 (2") center
square. Join into rows; join rows to
complete quilt center.

Inner Border Assembly

1. Join 2 (3"-wide) inner border segments and 1 (2" × 3") red rectangle to complete 1 inner border. Make 4 inner borders.

2. Add inner borders to sides of quilt center.

3. Stitch 1 white square to each end of remaining inner borders. Add borders to top and bottom of quilt.

6. Add white side outer borders to quilt center. Add top and bottom outer borders to quilt.

Finishing

1. Referring to *Sew Easy: Prairie Point Edging* on page 163, make 32 prairie points from the red 4¼" squares. Machine baste 8 prairie points to each side of quilt.

2. Layer backing, batting, and quilt top; baste. Quilt as desired. Quilt shown was stipple quilted in the white areas.

3. Follow instructions in *Sew Easy* lesson on page 163 to trim backing and batting and finish quilt edge.

DESIGNER

Lyndsay Sharratt is involved in many aspects of quilting. She not only designs patterns, but also owns her own machine quilting business, Lyndsay's Quilting Bug.✳

Pattern is shown full size for use with fusible web. Add ³⁄₁₆" seam allowance for hand appliqué.

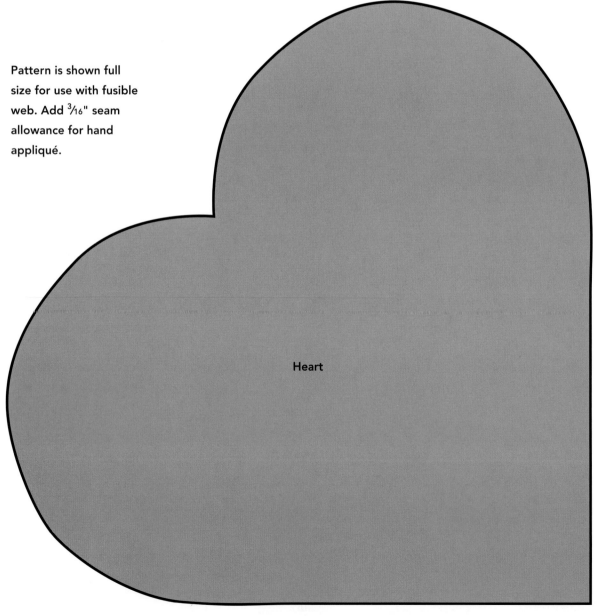

Heart

Sew Easy™
Prairie Point Edging

Folded fabric triangles, known as prairie points, are a fun alternative to traditional binding to finish quilt edges. Add prairie points to the quilt top before it is quilted. Follow the simple steps below to add this attractive edge finish to your quilt.

1. Cut squares of fabrics for prairie points. A good size for squares is 3½". These can be a variety of fabrics or all the same fabric. To estimate the number of squares to cut, assume that each prairie point will cover approximately 2½" to 3" of quilt edge. (For Crazy Hearts on page 160, cut 32 4¼" squares.

2. Fold each square in half diagonally, wrong sides facing; fold in half again to make a smaller triangle. Press (Photo A).

3. Align long raw edge of each prairie point with right side of fabric along edge of quilt top. Slip folded edge of each prairie point into open side of adjacent prairie point so they overlap

slightly (Photo B). Adjust spacing and overlap as needed so prairie points are spaced evenly around quilt top. At corners, position 2 prairie points with sides meeting. Machine baste prairie points to quilt top (Photo C).

4. After quilting is complete, trim backing and batting even with edge of quilt top. Trim away an extra ⅛"–¼" of batting. Turn prairie points so they face out from quilt top, bringing raw edge of quilt top and prairie points to inside.

5. Turn under ¼" on quilt back. Blindstitch folded edge of quilt back to prairie points to finish quilt edge (Photo D).

General Instructions

Basic Supplies

You'll need a **sewing machine (A)** in good working order to construct patchwork blocks, join blocks together, add borders, and machine quilt. We encourage you to purchase a machine from a local dealer, who can help you with service in the future, rather than from a discount store. Another option may be to borrow a machine from a friend or family member. If the machine has not been used in a while, have it serviced by a local dealer to make sure it is in good working order. If you need an extension cord, one with a surge protector is a good idea.

A **rotary cutting mat (B)** is essential for accurate and safe rotary cutting. Purchase one that is no smaller than 18" × 24".

Rotary cutting mats are made of "self-healing" material that can be used over and over.

A **rotary cutter (C)** is a cutting tool that looks like a pizza cutter, and has a very sharp blade. We recommend starting with a standard size 45mm rotary cutter. Always lock or close your cutter when it is not in use, and keep it out of the reach of children.

A **safety glove** (also known as a *Klutz Glove)* **(D)** is also recommended. Wear your safety glove on the hand that is holding the ruler in place. Because it is made of cut-resistant material, the safety glove protects your non-cutting hand from accidents that can occur if your cutting hand slips while cutting.

An acrylic **ruler (E)** is used in combination with your cutting mat and rotary cutter. We recommend the Fons & Porter

8" × 14" ruler, but a 6" × 12" ruler is another good option. You'll need a ruler with inch, quarter-inch, and eighth-inch markings that show clearly for ease of measuring. Choose a ruler with a 45-degree-angle line marked on it as well.

Since you will be using 100% cotton fabric for your quilts, use **cotton or cotton-covered polyester thread (F)** for piecing and quilting. Avoid 100% polyester thread, as it tends to snarl.

Keep a pair of small **scissors (G)** near your sewing machine for cutting threads.

Thin, good quality **straight pins (H)** are preferred by quilters. The pins included with pin cushions are normally too thick to use for piecing, so discard them. Purchase a box of nickel-plated brass **safety pins** size #1 **(I)** to use for pin-basting the layers of your quilt together for machine quilting.

Invest in a 120"-long dressmaker's **measuring tape (J)**. This will come in handy when making borders for your quilt.

A 0.7–0.9mm mechanical **pencil (K)** works well for marking on your fabric.

Invest in a quality sharp **seam ripper (L)**. Every quilter gets well-acquainted with her seam ripper!

Set up an **ironing board (M)** and **iron (N)** in your sewing area. Pressing yardage before cutting, and pressing patchwork seams as you go are both essential for quality quiltmaking. Select an iron that has steam capability.

Masking **tape (O)** or painter's tape works well to mark your sewing machine so you can sew an accurate ¼" seam. You will also use tape to hold your backing fabric taut as you prepare your quilt sandwich for machine quilting.

The most exciting item that you will need for quilting is **fabric (P)**. Quilters generally prefer 100% cotton fabrics for their quilts. This fabric is woven from cotton threads, and has a lengthwise and a crosswise grain. The term "bias" is used to describe the diagonal grain of the fabric. If you make a 45-degree angle cut through a square of cotton fabric, the cut edges will be bias edges, which are quite stretchy. As you learn more quiltmaking techniques, you'll learn how bias can work to your advantage or disadvantage.

Fabric is sold by the yard at quilt shops and fabric stores. Quilting fabric is generally about 40"–44" wide, so a yard

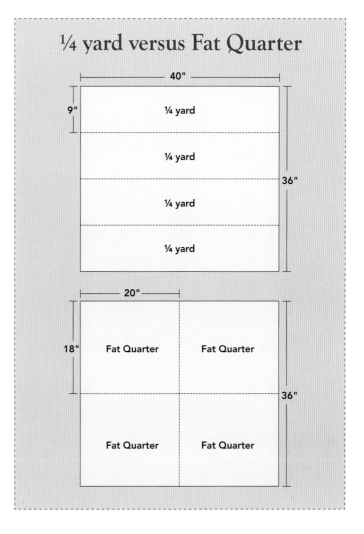

is about 40" wide by 36" long. As you collect fabrics to build your own personal stash, you will buy yards, half yards (about 40" × 18"), quarter yards (about 40" × 9"), as well as other lengths.

Many quilt shops sell "fat quarters," a special cut favored by quilters. A fat quarter is created by cutting a half yard down the fold line into two 20" × 18" pieces (fat quarters) that are sold separately. Quilters like the nearly square shape of the fat quarter because it is more useful than the narrow regular quarter yard cut.

Batting (Q) is the filler between quilt top and backing that makes your quilt a quilt. It can be cotton, polyester, cotton-polyester blend, wool, silk, or other natural materials, such as bamboo or corn. Make sure the batting you buy is at least six inches wider and six inches longer than your quilt top.

Accurate Cutting

Measuring and cutting accuracy are important for successful quilting. Measure at least twice, and cut once!

Cutting for patchwork usually begins with cutting strips, which are then cut into smaller pieces. First, cut straight strips from a fat quarter:

1. Fold fat quarter in half with selvage edge at the top (*Photo A*).

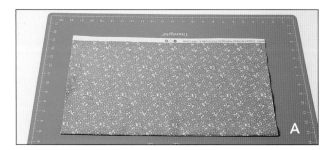

2. Straighten edge of fabric by placing ruler atop fabric, aligning one of the lines on ruler with selvage edge of fabric (*Photo B*). Cut along right edge of ruler.

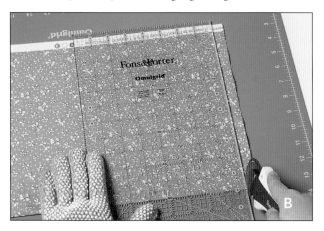

3. Rotate fabric, and use ruler to measure from cut edge to desired strip width (*Photo C*). Measurements in instructions include ¼" seam allowances. The Split Nine Patch requires 2½"-wide strips and 2⅞"-wide strips. Label strips as you go so they don't get mixed up (*Photo D*).

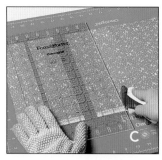

4. After cutting the required number of strips, cut strips into squares and label them (*Photo E*).

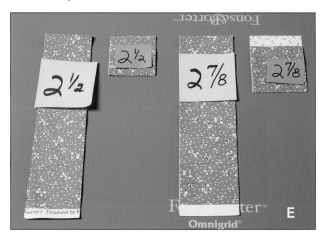

Setting up Your Sewing Machine

Sew Accurate ¼" Seams

Standard seam width for patchwork and quiltmaking is ¼". Some machines come with a patchwork presser foot, also known as a quarter-inch foot. If your machine doesn't have a quarter-inch foot, you may be able to purchase one from a dealer. Or, you can create a quarter-inch seam guide on your machine using masking tape or painter's tape.

Place an acrylic ruler on your sewing machine bed under the presser foot. Slowly turn handwheel until the tip of the needle barely rests atop the ruler's quarter-inch mark (*Photo A*). Make sure the lines on the ruler are parallel to the lines on the machine throat plate. Place tape on the machine bed along edge of ruler (*Photo B*).

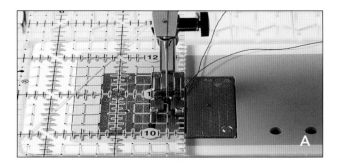

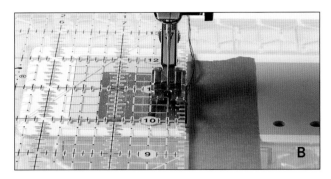

Take a Simple Seam Test

Seam accuracy is critical to machine piecing, so take this simple test once you have your quarter-inch presser foot on your machine or have created a tape guide.

Place 2 (2½") squares right sides together, and sew with a scant ¼" seam. Open squares and finger press seam. To finger press, with right sides facing you, press the seam to one side with your fingernail. Measure across pieces, raw edge to raw edge (*Photo C*). If they measure 4½", you have passed the test! Repeat the test as needed to make sure you can confidently sew a perfect ¼" seam.

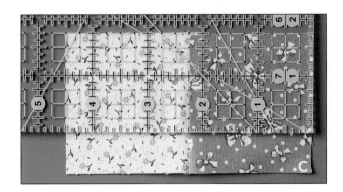

Sewing Comfortably

Other elements that promote pleasant sewing are good lighting, a comfortable chair, background music—and chocolate! Good lighting promotes accurate sewing. The better you can see what you are working on, the better your results. A comfortable chair enables you to sew for longer periods of time. An office chair with a good back rest and adjustable height works well. Music helps keep you relaxed. Chocolate is, for many quilters, simply a necessity.

Tips for Patchwork and Pressing

As you sew more patchwork, you'll develop your own shortcuts and favorite methods. Here are a few favored by many quilters:

- As you join patchwork units to form rows, and join rows to form blocks, press seams in opposite directions from row to row whenever possible (*Photo A*). By pressing seams one direction in the first row and the opposite direction in the next row, you will often create seam allowances that abut when rows are joined (*Photo B*). Abutting or nesting seams are ideal for forming perfectly matched corners on the right side of your quilt blocks and quilt top. Such pressing is not always possible, so don't worry if you end up with seam allowances facing the same direction as you join units.

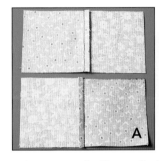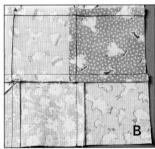

- Sew on and off a small, folded fabric square to prevent bobbin thread from bunching at throat plate (*Photo C*). You'll also save thread, which means fewer stops to wind bobbins, and fewer hanging threads to be snipped. Repeated use of the small piece of fabric gives it lots of thread "legs," so some quilters call it a spider.

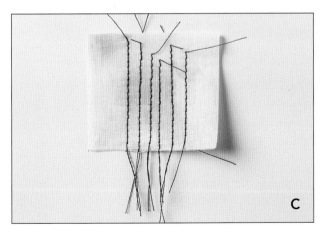

- Chain piece patchwork to reduce the amount of thread you use, and minimize the number and length of threads you need to trim from patchwork. Without cutting threads at the end of a seam, take 3–4 stitches without any fabric under the needle, creating a short thread chain approximately ⅛" long (*Photo D*). Repeat until you have a long line of pieces. Remove chain from machine, clip threads between units, and press seams.

- Trim off tiny triangle tips (sometimes called dog ears) created when making triangle-square units (*Photo E*). Trimming triangles reduces bulk and makes patchwork units and blocks lie flatter. Though no one will see the back of your quilt top once it's quilted, a neat back free of dangling threads and patchwork points is the mark of a good quilter. Also, a smooth, flat quilt top is easier to quilt, whether by hand or machine.

- Careful pressing will make your patchwork neat and crisp, and will help make your finished quilt top lie flat. Ironing and pressing are two different skills. Iron fabric to remove wrinkles using a back and forth, smoothing motion. Press patchwork and quilt blocks by raising and gently lowering the iron atop your work. After sewing a patchwork unit, first press the seam with the unit closed, pressing to set, or embed, the stitching. Setting the seam this way will help produce straight, crisp seams. Open the unit and press on the right side with the seam toward the darkest fabric,

being careful to not form a pleat in your seam, and carefully pressing the patchwork flat.

- Many quilters use finger pressing to open and flatten seams of small units before pressing with an iron. To finger press, open patchwork unit with right side of fabric facing you. Run your fingernail firmly along seam, making sure unit is fully open with no pleat.

- Careful use of steam in your iron will make seams and blocks crisp and flat (*Photo F*). Aggressive ironing can stretch blocks out of shape, and is a common pitfall for new quilters.

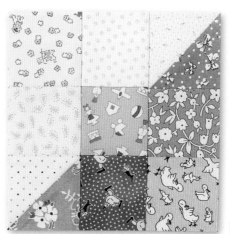

Adding Borders

Follow these simple instructions to make borders that fit perfectly on your quilt.

1. Find the length of your quilt by measuring through the quilt center, not along the edges, since the edges may have stretched. Take 3 measurements and average them to determine the length to cut your side borders (*Diagram A*). Cut 2 side borders this length.

2. Fold border strips in half to find center. Pinch to create crease mark or place a pin at center. Fold quilt top in half crosswise to find center of side. Attach side borders to quilt center by pinning them at the ends and the center, and easing in any fullness. If quilt edge is a bit longer than border, pin and sew with border on top; if border is

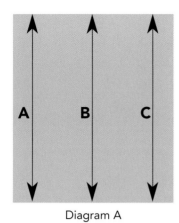

Diagram A

A _____

B _____

C _____

TOTAL _____

÷3

_____

AVERAGE
LENGTH _____

HELPFUL TIP

Use the following decimal conversions to calculate
your quilt's measurements:

⅛" = .125	⅝" = .625
¼" = .25	¾" = .75
⅜" = .375	⅞" = .875
½" = .5	

slightly longer than quilt top, pin and sew with border on
the bottom. Machine feed dogs will ease in the fullness of
the longer piece. Press seams toward borders.

3. Find the width of your quilt by measuring across the
quilt and side borders (*Diagram B*). Take 3 measurements
and average them to determine the length to cut your
top and bottom borders. Cut 2 borders this length.

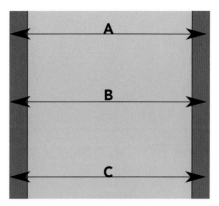

Diagram B

4. Mark centers of borders and top and bottom edges
of quilt top. Attach top and bottom borders to quilt,
pinnning at ends and center, and easing in any fullness
(*Diagram C*). Press seams toward borders.

Diagram C

5. Gently steam press entire quilt top on one side and then
the other. When pressing on wrong side, trim off any
loose threads.

Joining Border Strips

Not all quilts have borders, but they are a nice complement
to a quilt top. If your border is longer than 40", you will
need to join 2 or more strips to make a border the required
length. You can join border strips with either a straight seam
parallel to the ends of the strips (*Photo A*), or with a diagonal
seam. For the diagonal seam method, place one border strip
perpendicular to another strip, right sides facing (*Photo B*).
Stitch diagonally across strips as shown. Trim seam allowance
to ¼". Press seam open (*Photo C*).

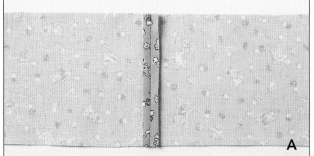

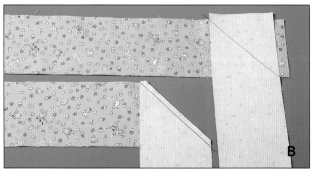

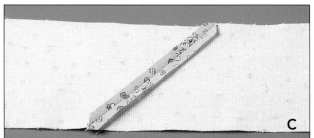

Quilting Your Quilt

Quilters today joke that there are three ways to quilt a quilt—by hand, by machine, or by check. Some enjoy making quilt tops so much, they prefer to hire a professional machine quilter to finish their work. The Split Nine Patch baby quilt shown at left has simple machine quilting that you can do yourself.

Decide what color thread will look best on your quilt top before choosing your backing fabric. A thread color that will blend in with the quilt top is a good choice for beginners. Choose backing fabric that will blend with your thread as well. A print fabric is a good choice for hiding less-than-perfect machine quilting. The backing fabric must be at least 3"–4" larger than your quilt top on all 4 sides. For example: if your quilt top measures 44" × 44", your backing needs to be at least 50" × 50". If your quilt top is 80" × 96", then your backing fabric needs to be at least 86" × 102".

For quilt tops 36" wide or less, use a single width of fabric for the backing. Buy enough length to allow adequate margin at quilt edges, as noted above. When your quilt is wider than 36", one option is to use 60"-, 90"-, or 108"-wide fabric for the quilt backing. Because fabric selection is limited for wide fabrics, quilters generally piece the quilt backing from 44/45"-wide fabric. Plan on 40"–42" of usable fabric width when estimating how much fabric to purchase. Plan your piecing strategy to avoid having a seam along the vertical or horizontal center of the quilt.

For a quilt 37"–60" wide, a backing with horizontal seams is usually the most economical use of fabric. For example, for a quilt 50" × 70", vertical seams would require 152", or 4¼ yards, of 44/45"-wide fabric (76" + 76" = 152"). Horizontal seams would require 112", or 3¼ yards (56" + 56" = 112").

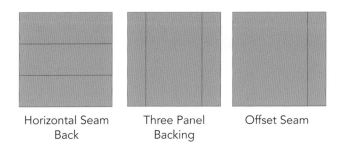

Horizontal Seam Back   Three Panel Backing   Offset Seam

For a quilt 61"–80" wide, most quilters piece a three-panel backing, with vertical seams, from two lengths of fabric. Cut one of the pieces in half lengthwise, and sew the halves to opposite sides of the wider panel. Press the seams away from the center panel.

For a quilt 81"–120" wide, you will need three lengths of fabric, plus extra margin. For example, for a quilt 108" × 108", purchase at least 342", or 9½ yards, of 44/45"-wide fabric (114" + 114" + 114" = 342").

For a three-panel backing, pin the selvage edge of the center panel to the selvage edge of the side panel, with edges aligned and right sides facing. Machine stitch with a ½" seam. Trim seam allowances to ¼", trimming off the selvages from both panels at once. Press the seam away from the center of the quilt. Repeat on other side of center panel.

For a two-panel backing, join panels in the same manner as above, and press the seam to one side.

Create a "quilt sandwich" by layering your backing, batting, and quilt top. Find the crosswise center of the backing fabric by folding it in half. Mark with a pin on each side. Lay backing down on a table or floor, wrong side up. Tape corners and edges of backing to the surface with masking or painter's tape so that backing is taut (*Photo A*).

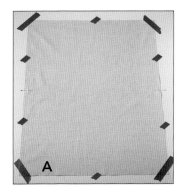

Fold batting in half crosswise and position it atop backing fabric, centering folded edge at center of backing (*Photo B*). Unfold batting and smooth it out atop backing (*Photo C*).

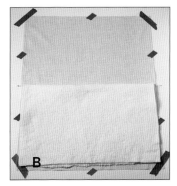 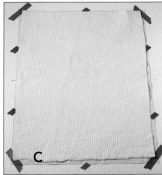

In the same manner, fold the quilt top in half crosswise and center it atop backing and batting (*Photo D*). Unfold top and smooth it out atop batting (*Photo E*).

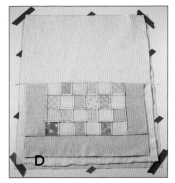 

Use safety pins to pin baste the layers (*Photo F*). Pins should be about a fist width apart. A special tool, called a Kwik Klip, or a grapefruit spoon makes closing the pins easier. As you slide a pin through all three layers, slide the point of the pin into one of the tool's grooves. Push on the tool to help close the pin.

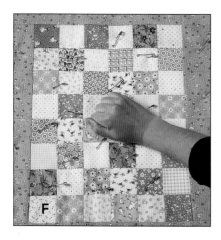

For straight line quilting, install an even feed or walking foot on your machine. This presser foot helps all three layers of your quilt move through the machine evenly without bunching.

Walking Foot

Stitching "in the ditch"

An easy way to quilt your first quilt is to stitch "in the ditch" along seam lines. No marking is needed for this type of quilting.

Binding Your Quilt

Preparing Binding

Strips for quilt binding may be cut either on the straight of grain or on the bias. For the quilts in this booklet, cut strips on the straight of grain.

1. Measure the perimeter of your quilt and add approximately 24" to allow for mitered corners and finished ends.
2. Cut the number of strips necessary to achieve desired length. We like to cut binding strips 2¼" wide.
3. Join your strips with diagonal seams into 1 continuous piece (*Photo A*). Press the seams open. (See page 169 for instructions for the diagonal seams method of joining strips.)

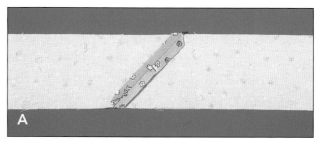

4. Press your binding in half lengthwise, with wrong sides facing, to make French-fold binding (*Photo B*).

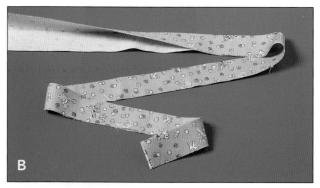

Attaching Binding

Attach the binding to your quilt using an even-feed or walking foot. This prevents puckering when sewing through the three layers.

1. Choose beginning point along one side of quilt. Do not start at a corner. Match the two raw edges of the binding strip to the raw edge of the quilt top. The folded edge

will be free and to left of seam line (*Photo C*). Leave 12" or longer tail of binding strip dangling free from beginning point. Stitch, using ¼" seam, through all layers.

2. For mitered corners, stop stitching ¼" from corner; backstitch, and remove quilt from sewing machine (*Photo D*). Place a pin ¼" from corner to mark where you will stop stitching.

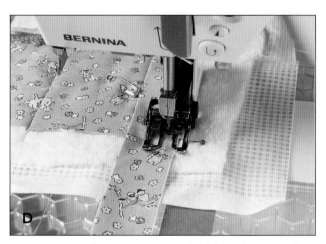

Rotate quilt quarter turn and fold binding straight up, away from corner, forming 45-degree-angle fold (*Photo E*).

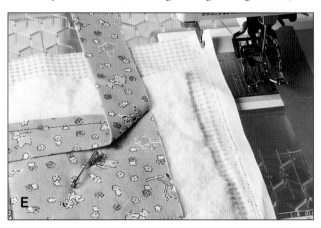

Bring binding straight down in line with next edge to be sewn, leaving top fold even with raw edge of previously sewn side (*Photo F*). Begin stitching at top edge, sewing through all layers (*Photo G*).

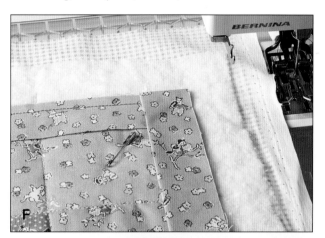

3. To finish binding, stop stitching about 8" away from starting point, leaving about a 12" tail at end (*Photo H*). Bring beginning and end of binding to center of 8" opening and fold each back, leaving about ¼" space

between the two folds of binding (*Photo I*). (Allowing this ¼" extra space is critical, as binding tends to stretch when it is stitched to the quilt. If the folded ends meet at this point, your binding will be too long for the space after the ends are joined.) Crease folds of binding with your fingernail.

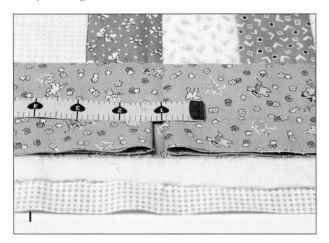

4. Open out each edge of binding and draw line across wrong side of binding on creased fold line, as shown in *Photo J*. Draw line along lengthwise fold of binding at same spot to create an X (*Photo K*).

5. With edge of ruler at marked X, line up 45-degree-angle marking on ruler with one long side of binding (*Photo L*). Draw diagonal line across binding as shown in *Photo M*.

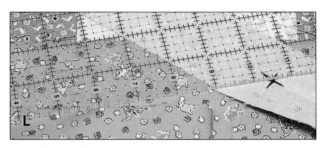

Repeat for other end of binding. Lines must angle in same direction (*Photo N*).

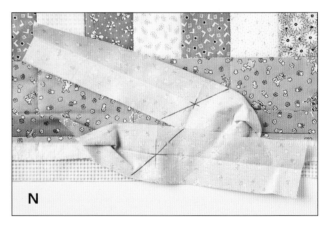

6. Pin binding ends together with right sides facing, pin-matching diagonal lines as shown in *Photo O*. Binding ends will be at right angles to each other. Machine-stitch along diagonal line, removing pins as you stitch (*Photo P*).

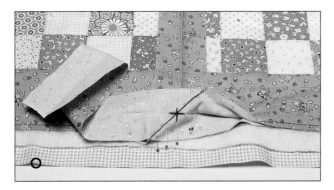

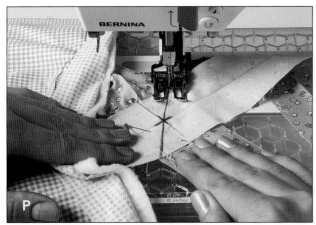

7. Lay binding against quilt to double-check that it is correct length (*Photo Q*). Trim ends of binding ¼" from diagonal seam (*Photo R*).

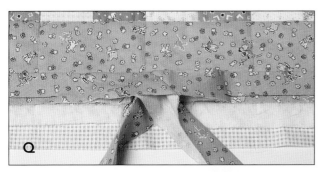

8. Finger press diagonal seam open (*Photo S*). Fold binding in half and finish stitching binding to quilt (*Photo T*).

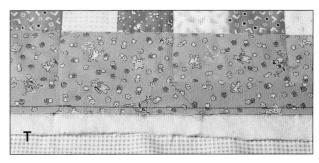

Hand Stitching Binding to Quilt Back

1. Trim any excess batting and quilt back with scissors or a rotary cutter (*Photo A*). Leave enough batting (about ⅛" beyond quilt top) to fill binding uniformly when it is turned to quilt back.

2. Bring folded edge of binding to quilt back so that it covers machine stitching. Blindstitch folded edge to quilt backing, using a few pins just ahead of stitching to hold binding in place (*Photo B*).

3. Continue stitching to corner. Fold unstitched binding from next side under, forming a 45-degree angle and a mitered corner. Stitch mitered folds on both front and back (*Photo C*).

Finishing Touches

- **Label your quilt so the recipient and future generations know who made it.** To make a label, use a fabric marking pen to write the details on a small piece of solid color fabric (*Photo A*). To make writing easier, put pieces of masking tape on the wrong side. Remove tape after writing. Use your iron to turn under ¼" on each edge, then stitch the label to the back of your quilt using a blindstitch, taking care not to sew through to quilt top.

- **Take a photo of your quilt.** Keep your photos in an album or journal along with notes, fabric swatches, and other information about the quilts.
- **If your quilt is a gift, include care instructions.** Some quilt shops carry pre-printed care labels you can sew onto the quilt (*Photo B*). Or, make a care label using the method described above.